By Mrs. Kemper Campbell

Here I Raise Mine Ebenezer
Whom God Hath Joined Asunder . . .
Marching Without Banners

Mrs. Kemper Campbell

❊

Marching Without Banners
AND OTHER DEVICES

SIMON AND SCHUSTER · NEW YORK

ALL RIGHTS RESERVED
INCLUDING THE RIGHT OF REPRODUCTION
IN WHOLE OR IN PART IN ANY FORM
COPYRIGHT © 1969 BY MRS. KEMPER CAMPBELL
PUBLISHED BY SIMON AND SCHUSTER
ROCKEFELLER CENTER, 630 FIFTH AVENUE
NEW YORK, NEW YORK 10020

FIRST PRINTING

SBN 671-20275-8
LIBRARY OF CONGRESS CATALOG CARD NUMBER: 70-75859
DESIGNED BY EDITH FOWLER
MANUFACTURED IN THE UNITED STATES OF AMERICA
AMERICAN BOOK-STRATFORD PRESS, INC.

This book is dedicated to four grandsons—David, Kemper, Craig, and Scott—in gratitude for their dedication to me.

Contents

WEARY OF BEING BITTER — 11
   Weary of Being Bitter — 13
   Furl the Banners — 15
   The Evil of My Ways — 18
   The Meaning of Loyalty, or Who Forgot the Flag? — 20
   A Kind Offer — 22
   Are Pride and Patriotism Inseparable? — 23
   Too Young to Serve — 24

ON MY LIST OF ANTIPATHIES — 27
   On My List of Antipathies — 29
   A Plague of Children — 30
   She Came Home — 31
   Two Wise Observations — 33
   With My Money Goes My Advice — 34
   The Story of the Clock — 35
   No Recruits — 38

WELCOME OMISSIONS — 41
   Welcome Omissions — 43

CONTENTS

So She Is Going Back to Paris	44
What Makes a Good Judge	46
Never Trust a Friend	48
The Tyranny of Machines	50

IMPORTANT MESSAGES — 53

Important Messages	55
The Dignity of Anger	56
Two Memorable Introductions	57
Incompetent Husbands	58
Best to Ignore It	60
A Hapless Blessing	61

IN CASE OF FIRE — 63

In Case of Fire	65
A Lover of Books	66
Do You Remember Him?	67
A Dirge for Poetry	69
An Embarrassing Gift	71
The Judge Who Could Make No Mistake	73

BEWARE OF POWERFUL WOMEN — 77

Beware of Powerful Women	79
Platonic Love	84
A Devoted Son	85
The Perfect Answer	86
A Valid Reason	87

A GOLDEN WEDDING — 89

A Golden Wedding	91
The Vacant Chair	92
Worn Smooth by Time	92
Not Recommended	94
Married Too Long	94
Breakfast	97
If You Mean Yes	98

CONTENTS

BOLD CHANGES IN EDUCATION — 101
- Bold Changes in Education — 103
- Right Over Right — 104
- Just in Time — 106
- Ashamed of America — 107

EVERY HOME NEEDS A GRANDFATHER — 109
- Every Home Needs a Grandfather — 111
- Let's Be Honest — 112
- Obedience — 113
- Uncertainty — 114
- Keep Them Busy — 115
- Clothes Make All the Difference — 117
- Grandmothers Are All Alike — 118
- A Parrot on His Shoulder — 119

VARIOUS WAYS TO BUILD CHARACTER — 121
- Various Ways to Build Character — 123
- Self-Reliance — 124
- Thrift — 124
- Learning to Spend Money — 125
- Lasting Happiness — 127
- Time to Be Generous — 128

PRESUME NOT GOD TO SCAN — 131
- Presume Not God to Scan — 133
- A Simplified Religion — 134
- Disbelief — 136
- The Beautiful Land — 137
- Living with a Handicap — 139
- A Christmas Story — 141

YOUR CARRIAGE, MADAME — 143
- Your Carriage, Madame — 145
- It Was All a Mistake — 146
- Salute on the Highway — 148

CONTENTS

Ambition — 149
My Only Claim to Fame — 151
How to Enjoy the Stock Market — 152
Another Prairie Chicken — 153

ON THE EDGE OF TIME — 155
On the Edge of Time — 157
Old People Live Too Long — 159
The Coward — 161
By Appointment — 163
Still Remembered — 164

THE RIVER IS SAFE — 165
The River Is Safe — 167
Forty Years Have Passed — 169
Ignoring the Depression — 170
Too Many Cooks — 171
Dogs — 175
Horses — 178
Spring — 182
Dust — 184
Flood — 187
Snow — 189
October — 191

❀ ❀ ❀

Weary of Being Bitter

Weary of Being Bitter

There is one cliché which, like so many of its kind, is utterly false. The saying goes, "Flattery will get you nowhere." The exact opposite is true. Flattery will get you everything from a chocolate cake to a husband.

I have just concluded a long and bitter feud.

Years ago a young Englishman who had trained close by for the R.A.F. wished to return here. I thought well of him. He had been cited for bravery during the war. With incredible strength and courage he had torn his co-pilot with the pilot's seat out of a flaming plane and carried him to safety.

When the war was over and won, he asked me to sponsor his return to Victorville. Such an act of kindness involves a complete revelation of one's morals, assets, income, and political affiliations. It is far easier to get a marriage license or borrow money from the local bank than it is to satisfy the United States government that you are sincere in what you say.

I promised to take care of the man for a year or until he

was able to support himself. This promise I kept from September until June. My friend partially paid his way by amusing me and greatly enriching my vocabulary. His choice of words was as remarkable as Lord Russell's, and his use of them was better. He was the only guest with whom I could read and enjoy Fowler's *Modern English Usage*. I enjoyed his sojourn in my home. Humor and the adequate word cannot, alas, be bought in the market place.

At last my friend fell in love with a girl who was both beautiful and beloved by us. From then on his success was consistent and assured. He has become the chief public-relations counsel for a large American firm. He travels from Vancouver to San Diego and from England to Australia, and his salary exceeds his needs.

But before he achieved this pinnacle of success we had a shattering misunderstanding. The details are best kept a secret. I am not tempted to make them a part of this story.

My final letter, which had better been unwritten, ended with the words, "You are not the sort of man who can forget a kindness. All the happiness you now enjoy is the result of what I did for you. Your ingratitude will hang around your neck like the dead albatross as long as you live." Alas, he had taught me the use of words all too well. My husband once said that I fortified my misunderstandings by pursuing them. It is true, and an explosive silence connected us for nine years.

I meant to forget him directly, but I found this hard to do while we so frequently repeated his wise and humorous sayings. Besides, among other things, he had left his vocabulary behind.

So things stood for nine years. At the end of that time he sent me a trade magazine in which he had written an article about me in the most glowing terms. It read:

Someone used the word *adobe* and a cloud of memories took me back three thousand miles to the Kemper Campbell Ranch in Southern California. You see, once upon a time I lived for many months on this ranch—months of bewilderment and infinite wonder, months in which somehow belatedly I learned finally to live.

As formidable in her way as the great ranch she owns was Mrs. Kemper Campbell herself. A woman of commanding presence and penetrating wit, she could undermine the toughest character with a word or a glance. Her judgments were summary and often witheringly, disconcertingly true. Even her misjudgments could be aphoristic.

Here was the old magic with words. He knew and he knew I would know that the statements were not true, but he had remembered my weakness. I am defenseless against flattery.

Nothing was said about forgiveness—a word that has no meaning for me. Only God can forgive. I am sure neither one of us will ever forget, but the scar is overlaid with mutual admiration. I had found a lost friend, and I was glad. I was weary of being bitter...

Furl the Banners

I am surrounded by Jeremiahs—both male and female. I am not a prophetess of doom. I have seen many improvements in my day. Causes for which I worked have for the most part succeeded, and many good causes have succeeded without my help.

I can remember when child labor laws were not universal as they are today. We often quoted the words of Sarah Cleghorn:

> *The golf links lie so near the mill*
> *That almost every day*
> *The laboring children can look out*
> *And watch the men at play.*

I wore out a pair of velvet shoes seeking signatures for the referendum and initiative. These laws have sometimes been abused, but they have done far more good than harm. They are guidelines which it is wise to respect. We are no longer at the mercy of the judges or the legislature. People forget that only in the last fifty years have we had the right to vote for our United States Senators; before that they were appointed and confirmed by the state legislature.

Birth control has become respectable. It was once against the law to send information through the mails. Even between doctors it had to go by express. This was due to the untiring efforts of Anthony Comstock, long since gone to his eternal reward. I wish Margaret Sanger, that tiny, fearless woman, could have lived to see the day when we are providing underprivileged nations with information at government expense. Last week the modified abortion law went into effect. It is no longer necessary to go to Mexico, Japan, or Sweden to avoid having a monster.

Even urban renewal is doomed. Not long will defenseless people be uprooted from their homes, driven out of their small businesses and compelled to dwell among strangers for the benefit of architects, contractors, plumbers and cement companies. Relief is on the way. California has passed a law providing that if fifty-one per cent of the people in an area sign a petition saying they do not wish to be "improved," they can stop the bulldozers in their tracks. It comforts me to know that when laws become so bad that they can get no worse, they always improve.

The Supreme Court of the United States has recently restored constitutional rights to juveniles. When I was head of the Juvenile Department of the District Attorney's office the reformation was in full swing. A boy or a girl could be convicted on the evidence of a postcard. It was not called conviction, but they were "taken into custody for their own protection." This is the age-old theory proclaimed by tyrants. We have reaped the whirlwind. Now that juvenile offenders are entitled to be confronted by the witnesses against them, to be represented by counsel, and to demand a jury trial, we can separate the guilty from the innocent. The guilty should be forced to work if they plan to eat. They are not entitled to a higher standard of living than the boys and girls who obey the law.

The Supreme Court has taken another long step in the right direction. It has decided that an officer of the law cannot enter a home without a search warrant. We are closer to the day when, as William Pitt said, "The poorest man may in his cottage bid defiance to all the forces of the Crown. It may be frail; its roof may shake; the wind blow through it; the storms may enter, the rain may enter—but the King of England cannot enter; all his forces dare not cross the threshold of the ruined tenement."

The Evil of My Ways

The members of the Republican club to which I belong are worried about only one thing—Communism. They are still reading papers about Marx and the Webbs. I don't know where Karl is buried, but the Webbs, man and wife, are both safely entombed in Westminster Abbey. I never knew why.

So I am left alone to worry about the injustice of urban renewal, the change taking place in our colleges, charity as a way of life, and other wrongs that should be corrected. I might as well throw split peas at Gibraltar. My friends are not concerned about anything outside of Russia and her influence.

If I say a kind word for the United Nations I am being deceived. If I suggest that Russia has improved since the days of Stalin I embark upon an argument which I can conclude only by suggesting that it is time to go home and leave me alone to consider the evil of my ways.

I am still of the opinion that Russia had reason to arrest two of our lieutenants while they were on a tour in that country. I sat by the father of one of the boys at a dinner in Washington last October. There was no question of their guilt. They had engaged in illegal transactions which they knew were against the law, and they had stolen an antique bear. They are both at home now after a jail sentence and a fine. Let's breathe a sigh of relief and resolve to behave ourselves when we are Russia's guests.

I may be called to testify before a congressional committee because I think the Russians are improving. There is greater freedom of speech, greater tolerance for liberal authors, and, best of all, a growing desire on the part of the Russian people to have something of their own. We believe that education is the hope of the world. The Russians are becoming educated. Are we wrong? If we are let's close our colleges and educate only a choice minority.

There are fundamental desires common to all men, and no government can permanently repress them.

I sat one day having lunch in a restaurant in Huntington Park. At the next table were two mothers and two children. A little girl was in a high chair. Beside her was a boy of five who insisted on putting his foot on the rung of her chair. She protested. The boy's mother said nothing. The mother of the little girl tried to persuade her to surrender.

Finally I stood up. "I am an attorney," I said, "and I propose to represent that child. The boy has no right and no reason to put his foot on the rung of her chair. Her objection is based on the Constitution of the United States and her inherent belief that she has certain rights and that one of them is the right to property. You can't brainwash that out of people, young or old. Russia has tried it, but she is failing—is sure to fail in the end."

The women looked surprised. It was quite a speech to make to two mothers who had only dropped in for a bite to eat.

The Meaning fo Loyalty, or Who Forgot the Flag?

The other night the Woman's Republican Club met at my house. Alas, they had forgotten to bring a flag. I was not at home, or I could have supplied them with one of my two flags. The women were bewildered. There was no way to open the meeting. It was as though the electricity had been turned off and they were left in total darkness. Finally they discovered on the wall of the dining room a plate commemorating our allies in the First World War. In the center of the plate was an American flag about the size of a postage stamp. The women reassembled in the dining room and pledged allegiance to the flag on the plate. Now all was well. The meeting was called to order and the secretary read her report. When I hear that pledge of allegiance, I wonder what people really mean.

The other day a guest at my dinner table said, "I do not believe in the two-party system. I am tired of these eternal fights every two years. I think we should do away with the two-party system."

At first I was too shocked to answer. Finally I replied, "You would have been happy in either Germany or Italy before the last war. They had only one party each."

When he pledged "one nation indivisible," did he misunderstand the word "indivisible"? Did he think it meant we should have no differences of opinion?

THE MEANING OF LOYALTY, OR WHO FORGOT THE FLAG?

"With liberty and justice for all." How do we propose to protect the liberty of which we boast? Are we thinking only of guns and planes and men in uniform? What about the grand jury? There is a movement afoot to discontinue it.

The grand jury is the only tribunal which has the legal right and duty to investigate every city and county official, including the judges. No wonder its members are threatened and maligned by the officials who are in danger. Not long ago a judge who was charged with instructing the grand jury at the beginning of their term warned them against making certain investigations. I wrote to all nineteen members of the jury and told them to disregard the judge's instructions. I wrote to the judge, and he admitted that he was wrong.

And what about that other jury—the twelve men who are sworn to decide on our guilt or innocence? I am dismayed when my friends ask me what I think of the jury system. Don't I agree that juries are stupid? What do they propose to take the place of the jury system—the Gestapo? In the words of Thomas Lambert, "The glory of the jury is its beautiful lawlessness."

Ever since the days of William Penn the jury has had a right to bring in a verdict contrary to the evidence if they disagree with the law and think it is unjust. In the early days of the eighteenth century many cruel and unjust laws were repealed because juries refused to convict. Some of these laws, such as the one which prohibited shooting a hare on the king's hunting grounds, carried a death penalty.

Let us include in our pledge of allegiance: "and to the jury which guarantees justice for all."

It was G. K. Chesterton who said:

Our civilization has very justly decided that determining the guilt or innocence of a man is a thing too important to be trusted to trained men. When it wants a library catalogued or a solar system discovered, it uses up its specialists. But when it wishes anything done that is really serious it collects twelve ordinary men standing about. The same thing was done, if I remember right, by the Founder of Christianity.

There is the story of the foreman of the jury who sent out for eleven lunches and one bale of hay. I have always had great respect for the man who got the bale of hay.

A Kind Offer

Our Woman's Republican Club cannot be held responsible if we are defeated at the polls. The members are untiring in their combined efforts. We have just concluded a garage sale. The garage was not for sale, but we each contributed something we did not want in return for something we did not need.

They devise various means for supporting the cause. These plans make a continuous chain of good works which stimulate our enthusiasm. I try to do my part.

Not long ago they held a cooky sale. My daughter volunteered six dozen cookies. It is customary for the oldest member of the family to bake the cookies..

It happened on the day of the sale that I had other duties to perform in addition to baking and delivering the cookies.

My daughter was meeting her husband's cousins from Italy, and she asked me to assemble a rug from the cleaner's and curtains from the dressmaker's and other items not to be forgotten.

It was four o'clock before I attempted to deliver the heavy box of cookies. By that time I was so worn out that I was a dejected object of pity.

I was told to deliver the cookies to the local pawnshop. I thought this strange, but concluded that we were meeting the enemy on his own grounds. I went to the shop only to find it locked. In my confusion I decided to try the bar next door. It seemed the logical step after the pawnshop. The lady bartender had no authority to accept the cookies. I turned wearily away, but help was at hand. An unkempt little woman who had been sitting at the bar followed me out. The joys of the afternoon and my age had touched her heart.

She tapped me on the shoulder. "Honey," she said, "Do you want to sell your cookies?"

Are Pride and Patriotism Inseparable?

Are pride and patriotism inseparable? I do not know. I rejoice in a competition that favors Los Angeles above San Francisco. I am loyal to the West as against the East, and I am downright unfriendly toward our nearest neighbor, the city of Barstow.

None of these prejudices is founded on principle or

righteous indignation. They are simply loyalties for which I have no defense.

Sometimes I am troubled by the part that national pride plays in national diplomacy. No war should be fought which has no higher motive than national pride. Many wars have been begun and carried on to final victory or defeat for no other reason.

I lost a brilliant son in World War Two. He wrote to me as early as 1938, "England will not sit by while the Germans exterminate the Jews. She will fight, and we must be found on her side."

When war came he volunteered. He believed in the causes for which we fought. His death was a great sorrow, but a sorrow free from bitterness. I harbor no resentment. But I would find death hard to accept in an undeclared war. I pity mothers who do not understand the causes for which we fight.

Too Young to Serve

Why is it that only the donkeys see the sword while the men in the saddle ride merrily on? If we must fight this thing called war, why do we first feed it until it all but destroys us?

Does anyone believe with the Irishmen that "it's a bad war but better than no war at all"?

I do not object to the draft. My two sons and my son-in-law volunteered in the last war. Two came back. But I do resent the fact that eighteen-year-old boys are drafted. They are too young. We allow a spirited horse to mature before we place a burden on him. We are careful not to breed a fine animal too soon. An eighteen-year-old boy is still a boy. We can afford to wait until he is a man.

It was a man named Stimson who was responsible for lowering the draft age to eighteen. I remember how it chilled my heart when Mr. Stimson told Congress that we needed these young boys for "spearheads."

We are a brave and loyal race. Long may our praise be sung. But must we defend ourselves with children?

❁ ❁ ❁

On My List of Antipathies

On My List of Antipathies

I am all o'er sib with zoning ordinances and building restrictions. These laws may do some good, but they do far more harm. They are a snare to the innocent and a bid for corruption.

The abatement laws are ample for our protection. They are universal and can be invoked anywhere in the United States against a nuisance which is dangerous to life or health.

I had an old neighbor who was a very successful farmer. He owned wide acres and a comfortable house set far back from the road. He gave me a sense of security I have not known since his death. I knew that if in this precarious world I should lose my uneasy fortune, I could go to him and be safe and welcome. He had room for us all.

The house had a downstairs bathroom, a modern bathroom with everything except a toilet. He said no toilet belonged in the house. It belonged halfway between the kitchen and the barn. I did not share his prejudice, but I believed in his right to live as he pleased so long as nothing he did interfered with the rights of his neighbors.

A Plague of Children

A marriage license should not entitle people to have children. Parenthood should demand a second license granted after careful examination and the approval of, say, a dozen friends and relatives.

I find it very easy to love one child at a time. But the older I grow the harder it is for me to endure children in depth.

This has been a holiday weekend, and we have had thirty-three children as guests. They have climbed the haystacks, swung on the aerials, and jumped into the well hole. It is not really a well, only a false well that the movies built for effect, but it was filled with hollyhocks about to bloom. The children stole the ping-pong paddles and wrecked some of the patio furniture.

The parents said it was such a relief to bring their children to a ranch where they could not get into any trouble.

If I had a few days I could easily ignore the parents and organize a course in basic training, and the children and I would part friends. But the time was too short. I could only suffer and pray for Monday morning (and be rude to the parents).

My family are wondering what to do with me. Am I

turning against children? Someone suggested that they take me to the shelter and advertise, "One good grandmother. Needs a home where there are no children. Has not had rabies shots."

She Came Home

I had a letter from the federal government asking me to help keep students employed during the summer months. We have more guests during the summer, so I decided to do as the government suggested. We have colored help and Mexican help, and we have three fine maids who were sent to us by the Welfare Department. I like to please the government when I can, although of late they have made almost no attempt to please me.

It happened that Jean went on a vacation in June and gave me the following list of instructions. After I read and reread it I decided not to hire additional help. It would only expose me to the danger of making more mistakes and incurring the wrath of the numerous departments with which I have to deal. Her instructions read:

DEAREST MOTHER:

This is a terrible time for me to be away from the ranch, because both the payroll and the quarterly returns will be due while I am gone. I hope the following instructions will make it all a bit easier.

Payroll: Pull out all the individual payroll folders for the

ON MY LIST OF ANTIPATHIES

individual employees. Remember that two are on the hourly wage and the rest on a monthly salary.

You will need the hourly schedule (two pages) that the girls fill out each day.

Add the hours worked in the rooms and multiply by $1.65. This amount is charged to column 311—hotel employment. We pay a different industrial-accident rate on this column (the rate is higher than the restaurant rate).

Subtract column 311 from the total monthly rate. Charge this to column 312—restaurant employment. These figures are necessary for the Workmen's Compensation records.

Using the daily work sheets, figure out how much should be added to the basic wage for food. Add $3.10 per day for all meals: $1.75 for mornings and $1.35 for evenings if they do not work all day.

Ask the girls for forms 4070 showing what tips they received. If the tips amount to more than $20 during the month, they must be added for the withholding tax. When you figure Social Security, add in the board and room if any, but when you figure state payroll tax, do not include tips. We do not pay Social Security tax on tips. Only the girls pay tax on this amount.

You now have the amounts to figure the deductions. See circular *Employers Tax Guide 1968*. It is in the bottom drawer of the desk.

Add monthly board and room and wages to figure state unemployment tax. Their contribution is one per cent of that amount. Our contribution is higher. [I love the word "contribution."]

If this tax amounts to more than $50 it must be sent in monthly. Even if it is less than $50 it must be itemized on the quarterly returns.

Add withholding tax (figured on wages and tips), Social Security tax (add everything in for this), and state unemployment tax (no tips). Subtract these amounts from the amount due the girls and make out their checks. If you add their tips to their wages in order to meet the minimum wage, which we have never done, you must pay sales tax on the tips.

Remember that two of the girls work as domestics for Donna and me part of the time and there is a different schedule for taxes for the hours they work for us.

Remember also that you must pay sales tax to the state for food given to the help, and above all remember when you send in the sales tax that you must tax the amount received for pasture or hay sold to horses, but there is no sales tax if it is sold to cows. If you need me I'll come home.

She came home.

Two Wise Observations

The other night I drove a hundred miles to hear Gerald Ford, the representative from Michigan. Gerald Ford in one sentence, brief as a telegram, said what it has taken Jefferson, Keynes, Mill, Veblen, Whitehead, and many other economists volumes to say. "Remember," he said, "a government that is powerful enough to give you everything you want is powerful enough to take everything you have away from you."

Our Governor continues to please me. His statements do not conform to political guidelines, and I fear for him when he says, "I do not think it is right and just that men who work should have to provide better medical care for idle men than they are able to provide for themselves." Many voters will take exception to this opinion. I was in the optometrist's office the other day. A man on relief was in the same office asking for his eighth pair of prescription glasses in a year. He simply cannot keep track of his glasses.

With My Money Goes My Advice

I agree that it is unjust to criticize an individual or a government unless you are prepared to offer a solution to the problem.

I am often asked what I would do about the vast sums of money we are spending on relief. My answer is that I believe everyone is entitled to food, clothing, shelter, and medical attention, but I do not think they are entitled to gin, color television, and two automobiles.

With my money goes my advice. This was true of my own children. When they no longer needed my money, they were no longer obliged to take my advice, but until that time came I told them how to spend the money. The same principle should apply to the recipients of charity. Their expenditures should be rigidly supervised and the money given them accounted for.

Furthermore, mothers with dependent children and pregnant women should not be encouraged to move from state to state simply because one state is more generous than another. To each his own. I know one mother of three children who came west for that reason. Her husband gave her the money to move. He reasoned that this state would furnish his family a better living than he was willing to provide, and, besides, California had a healthier climate. He was going to Alaska. He felt he had done right for his wife and three children by sending them to California.

We hire from five to seven maids on the ranch. Some are on partial relief; others are self-supporting. Not long ago we hired a woman who had come to California from the Middle West to obtain a more liberal allowance for her children. Her parents were glad to help their daughter make the change and thereby relieve themselves of any further responsibility.

The woman was a good worker, and the charities supplemented her salary. With her first month's pay she bought her thirteen-year-old daughter six rather expensive dresses. No one had the legal right to interfere, but I pointed out to her that never in my life had I had six new dresses at one time and that to buy six dresses for a growing girl was a shocking waste of money. A reasonable amount of state funds should have been subtracted from her next month's check. The woman needs a conservator.

The rule should be universal, from dependent mothers to impoverished nations: with our money goes our advice.

The Story of the Clock

I see by the morning paper that a judge from the Juvenile Court has advocated relaxing the laws against the use of marijuana. When he returns from Europe he is to be transferred to another court. He is a brave judge. I shall write and tell him so. I disapprove of marijuana, but we are losing the fight.

I rejoiced when the Eighteenth Amendment became law. Now I agree that it did much harm. It broke down the barriers against crime for a whole generation. Once one knows in his heart that he has committed a felony, even though he is never found out, he has marred his record and it is easier to commit the second offense.

I ponder this as I look at the clock on my desk which has marked my hours for forty-four years.

It happened when my sister was in dental college. Four of her classmates were caught with liquor in their car. The car was confiscated, and the boys were thrown into jail. A conviction would mean that they could never practice dentistry in California.

My sister brought them to me. I was touched by their plight. Two of them had worked to put themselves through almost three years of college. They faced disaster.

I did something I had never done before. It is known as "springing the jail." I went to the Federal District Attorney and used all my influence, ethical and otherwise. I pleaded for mercy and threatened reprisals. Finally the District Attorney let them go. I think he did it because he felt sorry for the boys, and not out of fear of me.

The boys tried to pay me, but I refused their money. I cleared my conscience by not accepting pay for an act which was contrary to my standards. So they all four came to visit me and brought me the clock. They became successful dentists and, so far as I know, respectable citizens. I have outlived all four of them. Only the clock and I are left to remember.

Reformers are loath to admit their mistakes. They are entrenched behind their sincere beliefs, and they never learn the lesson that you cannot make men good by passing laws against evil. I fear they are making the same mistake they made in the days of prohibition by outlawing marijuana.

I taught medical jurisprudence for fifteen years before the use of marijuana was illegal. Now it is a felony with punishment up to life imprisonment. The severity of the punishment is proof that the law is not effective.

Since it became illegal the use of marijuana is far more widespread. Why sentence a man to life imprisonment for selling marijuana, which is not habit forming and only mildly intoxicating and has never been known to cause cancer of the lungs? I am not advocating a law against the sale of tobacco, but laws to be respected must be consistent.

The argument against marijuana is that it leads to other things. So does everything else in life. What about marriage?

Advocates who defend the law claim statistics prove that dope addicts first used marijuana. They also probably drank coffee before smoking marijuana.

I received a postcard recently which stated as fact that every Communist in America had eaten a pickle at one time in his life.

Marijuana is getting publicity it doesn't deserve, and the publicity is increasing its use. The increase is alarming.

A woman was arrested for having marijuana growing in her garden. She pleaded innocent. She said a little bird brought the seed. "What happened to the little bird?" asked a small boy. "Oh, he got a job on television," the woman replied.

ON MY LIST OF ANTIPATHIES

No Recruits

This current academic rebellion reminds me of my own youth. I spent the years between twenty and thirty fighting for one cause or another. Most of these causes succeeded not because of my efforts, but because our generation knew what we wanted. We were intelligent and our leaders showed us the way to victory.

All that time I dressed as well as I could afford to dress. I took a bath every day. I kept up my classes in school, and I did not break my mother's heart.

When there was a lull in crusades, I married and settled down to raise and help support a family.

Now that I am eighty-two the crusades pass me by. I falter by the way and am confused about the issues. I have leisure, but I have no banner.

In the little town where I live there are no hungry or underprivileged children, no neglected old people. However, I can think of two causes which I might possibly support. One is a movement to reverse the policy in our state which provides that an illegitimate child is worth eight thousand dollars at six per cent interest. The other is the excessive cost of hospital care. But I can recruit no followers.

My husband and I were attorneys for three southern-California hospitals: Loma Linda, the Glendale Sanitarium, and the White Memorial Hospital. I know something about how hospitals should be conducted, and if my advice were asked I could reduce the cost substantially. For instance, when I left the hospital recently I was given some expensive toilet creams and powders and a new thermometer for which I had no use. And I found to my surprise that a clyster which was always given free as unwelcome routine now costs two dollars and thirty cents.

I resent having to give my age, my father's name, and my religion every time I return to the same hospital. Repetition costs money. I threatened to tell them on my next visit that I was a Moslem and my father was Genghis Khan. However, the doctor warned me that the last time a patient gave Genghis Khan as his father they sent his body to Outer Mongolia.

❀ ❀ ❀

Welcome Omissions

Welcome Omissions

One day a friend of mine was ill in bed. When the husband came down to breakfast, the new maid said gayly, "Guess what we have for breakfast?" "What?" asked the husband. "No cream," she replied. He was trying to lose weight, so he was pleased.

A guest and his wife had dinner at my daughter's house. He was very enthusiastic at breakfast the next morning. "We had a simply wonderful meal last night," he said. Food always holds my interest. "What did you have?" I asked. He thought a while. "No garlic," he replied.

Many a party has been improved by the guests who declined the invitation.

Mark Twain once said that any library was a good library that contained nothing by Jane Austen. I feel the same way about Hemingway.

Just so I enjoy a concert if I do not have to listen to de Falla's "Fire Dance" or Chopin's "Polonaise."

A friend and I attended the prize-winning play *The*

Homecoming. I could think of nothing good to say about the performance, but my friend, who sees only good in the theater, said, "But the silences were so eloquent."

So She Is Going Back to Paris

Hélène has just phoned to say she is going back to Paris to live. I am so sorry. I have learned to love her dearly. She and her husband came to us as refugees during the Second World War. Life will not be the same after she goes.

Hélène is not going back with the same husband who brought her from France. She has another husband, who is also French. I do not think I would enjoy being married to a French husband, but Hélène prefers them. She could have married an American, but she is devoted to this last husband.

I do not understand the French, from Hélène's first husband down to de Gaulle. There are too many kinds of Frenchmen.

When my daughter was only sixteen, I sent her to a school just outside Paris. It was an expensive school, but a very poor one—two baths a week, no heat from seven to seven, inadequate food and indifferent treatment. The American Ambassador was no help. I consulted Mr. Brunswig, who was the head of the local French colony. He was shocked to think I had sent a sixteen-year-old child to France alone.

"But don't you trust the French?" I asked.

SO SHE IS GOING BACK TO PARIS

"There are five kinds of French people. I trust my own kind," he replied.

The director of the school where I had sent Jean assumed incorrectly that I was far away and could make no demands. I wrote only one letter. I told her that her school had been recommended by the French consul in Los Angeles. I said that my daughter would have received better treatment if I had kept her at home and sent her to Juvenile Hall. Delinquent girls are treated very well in Los Angeles County.

I said that if she did not let my daughter go and return a just part of the year's tuition I had paid, I would write a letter to every French consul in the United States and tell the truth about her school. I pointed out that it would cost me only two cents a letter. That was before the postal rate went up.

Her reaction was immediate. She returned the money and made arrangements for Jean to go to Paris. The next months were happy ones. Jean attended the Sorbonne and lived with a remarkable French couple, Mr. and Mrs. Georges Monod, who treated her like a daughter. After thirty years she is still devoted to them.

She made many friends in Paris, among them Hélène. Hélène and her husband lived with us several months during the war. Antoine was an excellent conversationalist, and I enjoyed him, but I found him a hard man in a bargain. I never even won a compromise decision.

Hélène found work in town, and they rented one of our houses, which he furnished with the bare necessities.

When the Free French organized in America and asked for volunteers, Antoine volunteered to fight for France for the third time. He was training in the French Army when the First World War ended, he fought in the Second World War and escaped after France surrendered, and now he was going to war again.

My admiration was unbounded and I agreed to buy his furniture. I did not need it, and I especially did not want two imitation rag rugs. He assured me he could sell them to another friend.

Finally the day came for him to leave. He came to say goodbye. "How about the two rugs?" he asked. I said, "You know I do not want them, but because I admire your bravery I'll take them. How much are you asking for them?"

"I paid eighteen for one and twelve for the other," he answered. I gave him a check for thirty dollars. He walked away, apparently satisfied. Before he reached his car he turned and came back. "I forgot the sales tax," he said.

I am very sad that Hélène is going back to live in Paris. She is leaving Antoine in America. She will never miss him.

What Makes a Good Judge

It takes more than honesty to make a good judge. I have known men whose ethics I questioned appointed to the bench. I have seen them take their authority seriously and mend their ways and become upright judges.

But stupid men are not improved by advancement. Once a stupid judge, always a stupid judge. Authority only gives them more scope for their stupidity. Death alone can improve them.

WHAT MAKES A GOOD JUDGE

A good judge should have a restrained sense of humor. It acts as a buffer between him and the daily irritations he is paid to suffer.

There is the story of a judge who sat on the bench for many years. He is long since dead. His name was Waldo York. Even the name had a pompous sound. It was in the days before judges were in robes, and Judge York wore a coat that was split in the back, so that before sitting down he ceremoniously separated his coattails, thereby revealing a posterior of more than ordinary proportions.

One day as he performed this ceremony an attorney named Dell Sweitzer remarked to a friend sitting beside him, "All ass, poor York, I knew him well." The bailiff overheard the remark, and, like the judge, he was completely lacking in humor. He told Judge York. Judge York promptly fined Mr. Sweitzer five hundred dollars or ten days in jail.

Mr. Sweitzer gladly paid the fine. The joke quickly spread through the bar. The sitting ceremony was promptly discontinued.

On the other hand, an overconfident sense of humor can be quite as unfortunate. I once helped to elect a man who had an office in our suite. I had found him an enjoyable companion. I lived to regret my part in elevating him to the bench. His sense of humor was disastrous and was the cause of his undoing. He took advantage of his captive audience. Alas for the litigant whose attorney failed to laugh at the proper time. The Appellate Court tried to curb his levity, but without success. He was a total failure. Attorneys refused to appear before him.

He became so unpopular that he had to write his own eulogy and ask his bailiff to read it at his funeral. It was humorous all right, but no one laughed.

Never Trust a Friend

Never trust a friend for an amount that is more than you can afford to lose or for a time of payment that is long enough for him to forget.

Two young friends of mine started a store together. They had no articles of partnership. They began business with a handshake and continued on this basis for more than thirty years. Not long ago one of the partners died, and his handshake died with him. Now the store is in trouble, and the heirs are suing for an accounting.

I have known Frances for a very long time. I think I first met her when I helped settle her father's estate. I never met Peter until after they were married, but I liked him. He would have fit nicely into a Western novel just as he was. He came from New Mexico, and he was at home in the woods and on the mountains and always on a horse.

Peter's father died just as he finished high school, and he refused to go to college. He wanted to raise cattle. He had an unmarried uncle named Rodney who came to live with him after his father died, and as well as he could he took the place of Peter's father. The uncle worked in the local post office. When it became certain that Peter was not going to college Uncle Rodney offered to help him purchase a small herd of cattle—about twenty-five head, as I remember. Peter loved cattle and the life of a cattleman, and he worked very hard to increase the herd and prove to his uncle that he had made a wise investment. They spoke of the cattle business as a partnership, and all was friendly between them.

Peter did most of the work. Uncle Rodney helped on holidays and summer vacations, more for the pleasure of being on a horse than for any real service to the enterprise.

Soon after Frances married Peter she came to Los Angeles to visit with her mother, and we had lunch together. I was uneasy when she told me about Peter and his uncle and their loosely defined partnership. She said she had discussed it with Peter, but Peter had been firm about it. He said that he had perfect faith in his uncle and that since his uncle had no children the entire herd would belong to them when his uncle died. Soon after that Uncle Rodney came to live with Peter and Frances.

I met Peter a time or two, and once I mentioned the partnership. That was after their twin girls were born. I could see that Peter wanted no advice from me. The situation was complicated when Rodney married the first of his three wives and moved into a home of his own. The new wife loved Frances, and they became close friends. The first wife died, and Rodney married a second widow. She died soon after they were married, and Rodney went back to live with Peter.

Nothing happened for a span of ten years or more. Then Rodney married for the third time. This was a mistake. The new wife was a retired schoolteacher who had never been married before. Frances said that she thought Uncle Rodney was determined to find a wife who would be buried beside him. Two of his wives had asked to be buried by their first husbands. She said Uncle Rodney never liked to be alone.

The last wife was above accepting the duties of a domestic. Rodney came to Frances for many of his meals, and he always brought her his laundry. His wife took her laundry to town. Frances hoped that this disagreement would lead to a separation, but Uncle Rodney was not quick to give up the advantage of a wife who had had no former husband to interfere with his plans for his last resting place. Besides, he had grown old and senile.

Two years ago the partnership came to a sudden end. The new wife was vigorous and aggressive. She insisted upon dissolving the partnership. She threatened to leave poor Uncle Rodney. So he demanded his half of the business. He made no allowance for the fact that Peter had done all the work for thirty years. He took half of the herd, half of the saddles and the bits and bridles. Peter had to borrow fifty thousand dollars to pay Uncle Rodney for his share of the mountain pastures they owned. It was a great hardship. The twin girls are in college, and the third child, a boy, is in high school.

I met Frances this fall when she came to Los Angeles to borrow the fifty thousand from her mother. I asked her if she ever reminded Peter, "I told you so." I knew what her answer would be. "No," she replied. "He remembers."

Frances is being very casual about it. Her final remark was, "How thankful I am that I will never have to wash his dirty jeans again, and, besides, we have had our first Christmas dinner alone in more than thirty years."

The Tyranny of Machines

I question whether farmers lead easier lives now because of modern improvements. Certainly automation is not responsible for unemployment. My opinion, based on vast experience, is that every machine provides work for far more men than were required to do the job by hand.

Today happened to be just an average day. Something went wrong with one of the hot-water heaters, and it took two men to repair it with a part that took several men to manufacture. In my youth we heated water on the back of the wood stove at no extra cost of labor or material.

Then about noon the steam shovel working at the hospital on top of the hill broke our gas main, and it took several men all afternoon to turn off the stoves, the air conditioning, the hot-water heaters, and the clothes dryer, repair the gas line and turn them all on again.

The clothes dryer needed a new part, and a repair man was sent to fix it. The old clothesline on which we hung the washing for years never needed new parts.

Our plumber is very kind and comes to us in every emergency. He expects to come on either Thanksgiving or Christmas or both. On one of these days the bath water from a room upstairs ran into the tub of a guest below. You cannot blame the guest below for being reluctant to use this water of uncertain origin. Remember the washtub that stood in front of the kitchen range and could be filled and emptied at will?

There have been no complaints today about the dishwasher and the garbage disposal, but there is a standing army in town ready to repair them. I can wash dishes by hand, and garbage has its uses.

Surely every modern appliance has provided work for its quota of men.

I drive a car with some assurance, but I never tamper with any of the gadgets added to cars every year. I tried using these improvements on one car we owned, and I was finally forbidden to drive the car, in order to save my life.

When I bought this last car I was urged to have a button installed that would, of all things, open the trunk in the back. I can imagine what would happen if I drove along the freeway with the trunk cover up in the air like a sail. The salesman also recommended some arrangement to lock the accelerator and relieve me of the duty of obeying the traffic laws. All this I refused. I told them to point to the starter and the brake, and I would take it from there.

Once a garage man showed me how to unscrew the gas line and blow through it or put a cold cloth around a circular metal can under the hood. When the car stalled I tried one or both of these procedures, and they sometimes worked. But I never knew why.

I was like the man in Barstow whose duty it was to tap the wheels of the trains when they reached the end of the division. Someone asked him why he did it, and he replied, "I don't know. They never told me."

The foreman just knocked at my door to tell me that the electric pump had stopped. Oh, for the old oaken bucket!

It is unfortunate that we are losing our ability to improvise. A few months ago I attended a wedding. The church was filled, and the bride waited. The groom was nearly an hour late. His family lived a long distance out of town, and the electricity failed. He could not use his razor.

❋ ❋ ❋

Important Messages

Important Messages

Arthur Brisbane once told me that in spite of the fact that he had received hundreds of messages by wire, a telegram never failed to frighten him. Most people have the same fear. It is a relief to open a telegram and find that it is not a death notice.

When Joe was in high school the maid sent me one such telegram: "Joe wins second in national essay contest. Has slight case of impetigo."

Sometimes we receive welcome thank-you notes over the wires. We sent a friend east by train. She had enjoyed avocadoes for the first time, so we presented her with a box as we said goodbye. Later we received a telegram which read, "Arrived safely in New York. Avocadoes all spoiled. Thank you very much."

We are in the habit of including with our Christmas cards a recipe which our friends have requested. Each year we receive a reply from one guest thanking us for our kindness but suggesting an improvement or omission. This has been going on for some time. (We do not welcome suggestions for improving anything on the ranch. We have to live here.)

A year ago we gave the world the benefit of our chocolate-soufflé recipe, of which we are very proud. It is one of the two or three things of value which Jean brought home from a year in Paris.

In return we received a letter asking, "Haven't you forgotten the milk?" My daughter-in-law replied by wire. Her telegram was brief. "No," it read.

※

The Dignity of Anger

I respect the dignity of anger.

When one has a real grievance there are two methods of protesting. If the person responsible for the injustice is far away a letter written in the heat of passion is the answer. If the offender is close at hand a simple question may solve the problem. "What is your number?" is very effective. I have used this method with success on several occasions.

Last night a long freight train pulled over our crossing. It was just at dinner time, and the men coming in from the field waited for more than an hour.

It was time to do something. I put on a formal suit and drove down to where the engine was standing. I walked up to the track and asked the engineer why he did not break the train at the crossing.

"Lady," he said firmly, "we can't break this train."

"What is your number?" I replied. "I shall call the division superintendent."

The engineer was reasonable. He said that if I would take a brakeman back to the crossing he would let the men go through to dinner.

Once when I was coming out from under an anesthetic after a serious operation, the nurse who was giving me a saline solution dropped the metal container. It made a dreadful noise. I opened my eyes and demanded, "What's your number?"

My son, who was sitting by my bed, was immediately reassured. "She is all right," he said.

Two Memorable Introductions

Much eloquence, good and bad, is wasted on introductions. They should be either restricted or discontinued. I have heard only two introductions among hundreds which were worth remembering.

The first was when William Jennings Bryan spoke in Los Angeles. Mary Foy was on the National Democratic Committee, and she was given the honor of introducing him. The vast Philharmonic Auditorium was crowded. Mary Foy was a large woman, and she walked with a light side-to-side motion which gave the impression that she was being wheeled on a dolly.

She wheeled herself slowly to the front of the platform and waited. The silence was profound. Then she said, pausing after each word, "Ladies—and—gentlemen, William—Jennings—Bryan." With that she wheeled herself to the back of the stage and sat down.

The other introduction was at an American Bar Association convention held at the Palace Hotel in San Francisco. There were a number of famous after-dinner speakers, among them John Davis—who had been ambassador to the Court of St. James's—Lord Shaw of Scotland, and, last of all, Chief Justice Taft.

The honor of introducing Justice Taft was given to a leader of the San Francisco bar who was a noted wit. I withhold his name in deference to his family. He died long ago. No doubt he appreciated the importance of the occasion and fortified himself with a drink or two before dinner and now and again as the evening progressed. It was unfortunate. He rose and started to speak. Those present variously estimated the time he took for the introduction. Some say it was an hour, although it seemed longer. I think the official record was forty minutes.

When he had finished, Justice Taft stood up, "Mr. President, ladies and gentlemen, and members of the bar," he began, "I do not intend to deliver today the speech I had prepared for yesterday." And he sat down.

Incompetent Husbands

My husband never acted as a domestic or a handyman. Once he volunteered to shell peas when I was very busy. He did an excellent job, and I complimented him on a task well done, but I never asked him to do anything more complicated.

Men with the best of intentions but no talent have done irreparable harm in their willingness to be helpful. There was Edward Ryan. Mr. Ryan was very efficient on the moving-picture sets, and he offered to help me out of a serious dilemma. My nephew had wired our houses together in a handy communication system. I could turn a dial and hear what was doing in the main living room or in the home of either of my children. I was pleased with this convenience, but it met with the stern disapproval of the rest of the family. They were unanimous in protesting this invasion of their privacy.

Mr. Ryan said he could fix the system so that the family could turn it off in each of their homes if they wanted to be out of touch with me. I reluctantly consented to let him try.

He worked hard all day and when he was ready to go home he said, "Well, it's fixed. When you turn it off the lights go on and the toilets flush." He had solved the problem, for it never worked again.

One of my most successful friends has finally been persuaded by his wife to forgo a career as a handyman. Although he progresses from one vice-presidency to another, he has a fixed idea that it is more manly to work with one's hands—all men should be proficient at manual labor.

His last endeavor met with his wife's jaded disapproval. She had selected a piece of expensive linoleum for the bathroom floor. She had used some of her Christmas money to buy exactly what she wanted. Her husband volunteered to lay it. They are happily married and his wife is cautious of her husband's feelings, so she let him lay the linoleum one Sunday morning. He carefully drew the pattern of the utilities in the bathroom. Then he turned the linoleum over and drew the pattern on the back side. When he cut it out all the openings were reversed. The result was disappointing.

My lawyer once told me a story of his brother-in-law. He said that his sister was continually boasting that her husband was useless around the house, no good with a paintbrush, couldn't repair a switch or stop a leaking faucet.

Finally her husband said to her, "Listen, my dear, we have been married twenty-five years. All this time you have been pointing out the fact that I am a failure as a handyman. I have never denied it or tried to improve my standing. Now I want to tell you something. I have made a comfortable fortune in the grocery business. We have no children. I am leaving everything to you, and, like all husbands, I shall die first. When I am gone you will be a rich widow and you can marry any damn plumber you choose."

Best to Ignore It

Except in the interest of public morals, I never tell anyone what is wrong with their clothes. I am not grateful to be told that I have a run in my stocking unless I am on my way to the opera, which is seldom.

What if an underskirt is too long? It is not a matter of public concern, and I choose to ignore it. The underskirt can lead to no disaster. It will not contribute to an automobile accident, spread disease or kindle a fire. And the time involved in changing the skirt may cause the owner to miss a bus.

I have a car with lights that turn off automatically when I am in the house. My current amusement is to wait for one friend after another to tell me I have left my lights on. It reminds me of the man who bought a horse for fifty dollars. When the seller asked him where to deliver it, he said, "Put it in the bathroom." "In the bathroom!" "Yes, in the bathroom. I am having a houseful of company this weekend, and each guest in turn will come to me and say, 'You have a horse in your bathroom,' and I can reply, 'I know it.'"

Once a friend of mine and her sister were walking down a street in New York. It was in the days before the invention of the zipper. My friend said to her sister, "That woman's placket is open. I am going to tell her."

The sister replied, "Oh, don't bother. She wouldn't care anyway. Look, her heels are all run over."

But my friend, ever on the alert to do a kindness, persisted. She caught up with the woman, tapped her on the shoulder and said, "Pardon me, lady, but your heels are all run over."

A Hapless Blessing

A friend has just given me four wonderful pencils. Nothing pleasures me more than a pencil that shows a willingness to write.

Many years ago as my father was walking down the

railroad track on his way home from work he found a box containing a gross of pencils. He assumed that they had fallen off the train, but I always thought they had been thrown off by some exasperated clerk who had tried to write with one.

That was before the state furnished students with all necessary supplies. One hundred and forty-four pencils were enough to arm three daughters through high school, and my mother was grateful. But those pencils were composed of the hardest lead ever mined in the United States. Writing with them was an endless battle between the pencil and the paper.

I shall never know what success I might have achieved in high school with a pliant pencil. As long as I could remember I had enjoyed writing, and not only that, I had enjoyed reading what I had written. But those unrelenting pencils thwarted my ambition.

I was past seventy when I again had the urge to write. By that time I was able to afford soft pencils.

❈ ❈ ❈

In Case of Fire

In Case of Fire

A primitive fear possesses most of us in case of fire. Homes and lives are lost because even sensible people cannot face up to the emergency. Everyone knows the oft-told story of the men who carried mattresses downstairs and threw mirrors out the window. I plan to save the children's baby pictures and my few heirlooms and precious antiques. Perhaps not. I will wait and see when the time comes. I knew a grand old lady who cautioned her children nightly, "If the house takes fire grab something off the bed so whatever happens you will not be seen in your night clothes."

Many of our friends lost everything in the recent Bel-Air fire. I asked one of them what he minded most. I expected him to say the old grand piano. The piano had known the touch of famous pianists during its career on the concert stage. Alas, it was not the piano for which he mourned. He had just mated two rare orchids, and now he would never know what beautiful flowers might have resulted from this greenhouse marriage.

Another victim of the same fire saved her checkbook. She was proud that her checkbook was always balanced in case of disaster. "Now I will not be out of money," she boasted.

※

A Lover of Books

It must have been forty years ago that I first noticed a tiny bookstore on West Eighth Street. It was no larger than the bookstalls on the east bank of the Seine. It was there I met the man who was the owner and the entire staff of the little store.

I had the good fortune to pass his stand twice a day as I walked from the garage to my office. I often stopped to browse through the books on my way home from work.

Shortly, very shortly, after I first met Louis Epstein came that Friday when between our morning greeting and our evening farewell the stock market crashed with a sound heard in every city in the world. The disaster closed many stores along the street, but not the tiny bookstore. It must have affected him, but I never heard Mr. Epstein mention the depression.

Together we found our way through the seven lean years. When I could no longer afford a new coat, I could stop at night and buy a secondhand book to cherish. We shared the same bastion—the love of books. When banks fail and taxes threaten our land and houses, books remain and raise us above despair, even as Citizen Bratteaux escaped the terrors of the French Revolution by reading Lucretius.

Louis Epstein prospered and decided to move to Hollywood. I disapproved of the move. I predicted that, like so many men, Mr. Epstein was leaving a successful small business to fail in a larger business. Besides, I would miss him and his store.

I was wrong about the move to Hollywood. The Pickwick Bookshop is the second-largest bookstore in the United States. Once when I was in that vast store I looked at the thousands of books that crowd its shelves, and I asked, "Mr. Epstein, are these books *all* yours?"

"Yes," he answered modestly, "they are all mine."

He could have added, like Mr. Birrell, "These are mine and I am theirs."

Do You Remember Him?

He was intelligent, well-educated and prosperous. He bore a simple name like Ben. He may have been distantly related to Abou ben Adhem, for he was always involved in well-doing. He helped build a cathedral, he opened college doors, his home had a consulting room. Men and women came and laid their troubles on his dining-room table. He helped them order their lives.

He believed in an orderly world. Irregularities annoyed him. Once I visited him in one of those beautiful apartments overlooking the Golden Gate. In my bedroom was a curious square made by driving sixteen large nails in four perfect rows. I asked his wife whatever this strange design might mean.

"My husband cannot stand a floor that squeaks," she replied. "That was his way of repairing it." Fortunately he owned the apartment.

He liked to cook and was proud of his collection of rare cookbooks. But he did not believe in inspirational cooking. By following directions he sometimes became confused. I remember one dinner when he was having some difficulty carving a leg of lamb. He had inadvertently turned a page and was reading the directions for carving a turkey.

Once when his wife was ill he volunteered to cook the Sunday dinner. Again it was a roast leg of lamb. The wife kept smelling the lamb. Something was wrong in the kitchen. He assured her everything was all right. He had followed directions faithfully.

Finally she rose from her bed and slipped into the kitchen. The lamb was in the oven resting on the grate without a pan to protect it. "But," my friend said in self-defense, "the recipe said nothing about a pan."

In the Second World War he was the executive officer on a naval vessel. His ship was secretly known to be expendable. He survived the battles, but he barely survived the Admiral's wrath.

It was hot in the South Seas. It was like this man to find a way to make his men more comfortable. He had saved some sturdy boxes which had been used for ammunition. He sent in a requisition asking to be allowed to cut holes in the ship's sides and use the boxes for frames to provide more portholes. The Admiral signed the requisition among many other requests on his desk.

Later when they were both in the same port, the Admiral's voice boomed across the water. "Who in hell has those square portholes?" He sent for my friend. My friend brought the requisition with him. "But you signed it, sir." For the duration of the war his ship was recognized whenever it came into port—the only ship in the American Navy with square portholes.

The story ends. He died in an automobile accident last August. He left us with a better world.

A Dirge for Poetry

Lawrence Spingarn and his wife left today. Mr. Spingarn is a poet better known in England than in America. I had enjoyed his poetry and had clipped several of his poems from magazines before he published his three volumes of verse.

I still reread Mr. Spingarn's early poems, "Capital City," "We hear the thin rain tired of falling," and "Song of Myself," which tells how after his father died his sister reminded him, "Our flocks need tending now," and so he says:

> *I have no moments of regret*
> *For those my passion did beget:*
> *I wonder what the town would say*
> *Had passion flowed the other way?*
> *There is no substance in a song.*
> *No roof can rise above a rhyme.*
> *Perhaps the Muse will prove me wrong*
> *So more of this some other time.*

Or listen to his "Fever Fallen":

> *Oh, take me from this man:*
> *I've loved him all I can.*
> *My heart was free and wild*
> *When he was but a child.*
> *Alas, how could I know*
> *How soon mere children grow.*

These poems I understand. His later poems only confuse and frustrate me. I asked him the reason for the change. He answered me that only obscure poetry finds a market today. I replied that no poetry being written now was worth publishing, or perhaps it would be better to say that no poetry being published today was worth writing.

There was an article in a recent *New York Times Book Review* section on the new poets. It was written by M. L. Rosenthal. I quote one paragraph: "By negative feed-backs Alvarez meant the reactivation of the anti-experimental, anti-intellectual and anti-emotional sets or prejudices in English sensibility." If anyone knows what Mr. Rosenthal means will he please raise his hand?

Poetry is meant for everyday use, like bread and wine. It should be easily understood by scholars and common men alike. It should lighten the heart, it should set words to sorrow as Shakespeare and the Bible do.

Yesterday it snowed, and half a dozen guests greeted me in the morning with:

> *The snow had begun in the gloaming*
> *And busily all the night*
> *Had been heaping field and highway*
> *With a silence deep and white.*

"The First Snow Fall" was written before I was born more than eighty years ago, and every snowstorm since that day has reminded thousands of people of those simple, meaningful words.

I asked Mr. Spingarn if he thought Longfellow could find a publisher for *Evangeline* today. He replied, "Certainly not."

What modern poet can offer the comfort to the grieving heart of these lines by Robert Louis Stevenson:

> *Yet, O stricken heart, remember, oh, remember*
> *How of human days he lived the better part.*
> *April came to bloom and never dim December*
> *Breathed its killing chill upon the head or heart.*

An Embarrassing Gift

I have at last succeeded in giving my portrait away. It was sitting on the floor in the office when a guest admired it. I told her she could have it. She was simply delighted, and I hastened to wrap it up before she could change her mind.

What to do with this picture has been a problem for years. It was painted by a good commercial artist who was living on the ranch. She said I was a type or a study or something not quite normal. At first I declined, but the artist insisted on painting me. Finally I reluctantly consented. I took no interest in the work, and the picture showed it. I suppose that in order for a painter to paint a masterpiece the subject has to light up. I remained unnaturally dull. The dress I wore was beautiful, but only my four-year-old granddaughter viewed the finished portrait with enthusiasm.

I have never known anyone to be happy with a portrait painted by a living artist. President Johnson was displeased with his, and I am sure the artist did his best. There is something unpleasant about seeing yourself as the artist sees you. I have read that even Mr. Montgomery was disappointed with Sir Joshua Reynolds' portrait of his daughters as the Three Graces.

Some unpleasant portraits have achieved immortality. King Charles must have liked the works of Vandyke, and the King of Spain was evidently satisfied with Velázquez. I was afraid that mine would hang around the house, attic to basement, office floor to dark closet, until long after I was dead, and would become an example of bad art. So I brought it out of the attic a few days ago, intending to send it to a rummage sale for the Republican Party. Someone might buy it for the canvas. There was nothing wrong with the canvas.

But my family objected to displaying it in public even for a cause to which they are devoted. Perhaps they recoiled from exposing me to "public scorn and obloquy." So it remained on the office floor until rescued today by this kind friend.

I took her, together with my portrait, and saw them deposited on the overland train. I hope they arrive safely far, far away.

The Judge Who Could Make No Mistake

I have known scores of judges more or less intimately, and with two exceptions I have had complete confidence in their integrity.

One judge was guilty of such minor offenses he could hardly have merited the approval of the Devil. I first mistrusted him when he was shooting ducks on our ranch. He stole a duck that belonged to another hunter, and it was a male mallard. He was convicted of a lesser crime—accepting the bribe of a suit of clothes. He was recalled and died in obscurity.

The other case was a tragedy in which many people were involved. To protect his descendants I shall call him Judge Webb. He had befriended me through law school, encouraged me when I began to practice law, promoted my romances and officiated at my marriage although he had pleaded the cause of another suitor. He was like a father to me.

I once invited him to a house party, and I suggested that he bring his tennis racket. He replied that he was a Presbyterian and never played tennis on Sunday. I should have been warned.

Sometime later he took Kemper and me out to lunch. By that time he was a justice of the Appellate Court—the youngest member of the court. During the lunch he remarked that he was two hundred and fifty thousand dollars in debt. He did not appear worried, and he showed me some poetry he had written.

After we parted Kemper said that an Appellate Court judge had no right to be two hundred and fifty thousand dollars in debt. I said that no Appellate Court judge should write poor poetry. This was in the early Twenties, and the judge's salary was eighteen thousand dollars a year; that amount should have been adequate.

I tried not to worry about the incident and continued to maintain my faith in him. In fact, I planned to name my younger son for him. This was not to be. I deleted his name from the list of my intimate friends one morning when I saw him coming out of an apartment house. It was raining, and he was sharing an umbrella with a strange woman, or rather he was protecting the woman while he walked in the rain. I knew Mrs. Webb, and she was not the woman under the umbrella. I thought of the pious Scotswoman who said, "I will no' break the Seventh Commandment on Sunday." It was Wednesday morning.

This friendship ended badly. One day the secretary of the Bar Association's Grievance Committee showed me a letter which Judge Webb had written to the lady under the umbrella. She had complained that the judge owed her ten thousand dollars which he was making no effort to repay. In the letter the judge asked the question "Was not our love worth more than ten thousand dollars to you?" The answer was, "No."

This letter changed my friendship to contempt, but I still hoped to save him from final disaster for the sake of his innocent family and the trusting public. I am grieved when a public official deflects from the line of duty, and especially when it involves the very source of justice.

So I went to Judge Webb's chambers. I told him that he had held a place in my heart that no one else could fill, but that it would soon be empty. I said I could see the footprints of the people who were entering his chambers from the back door. I said, "I want you to know that although I shall never forget your kindness, I can no longer pose as your friend." Tears came to his eyes, and he assured me that I was mistaken.

It was not long before he was arrested. I was never quite sure whether the bribe was given or taken, but marked money had changed hands. My husband wept when he heard the verdict of the jury. Judge Webb's action had a lasting effect on the community. It shook people's faith in the integrity of the courts, which is a great pity, for the vast majority of the judges are worthy of respect.

After the trial and pending the appeal, the judge sent an emissary to ask me for money for his defense. I gave her money twice, but the third time I refused. I mistrusted her, and I told her if Judge Webb wanted more money he would have to ask me personally. He wrote me a bitter letter in which he said that he had always befriended me. I replied that I was not refusing my help, but I said, "You gave me the best advice I ever had. I gave you equally good advice. The difference is I took your advice and you ignored mine."

Judge Webb served his sentence. His mother-in-law converted the attic of her house into an apartment, and there he died. His mother-in-law had never liked him. He did not deserve this final indignity.

I am sure he died feeling that he had made no mistakes. His whole career was built on his immutable self-confidence.

I named my son Joseph. Joseph's moral reputation was above reproach.

❀ ❀ ❀

Beware of Powerful Women

Beware of Powerful Women

I have known three powerful women. Two of them ended in stark tragedy. I have lost all track of the third, but I am sure no good came of her.

When I was appointed a Deputy District Attorney I was introduced to a woman of standing and advised that it would be well to court her friendship. Instead she courted mine. She asked to be assigned to me as my investigator and so occupied the room next to mine. Then a friend warned me of the danger. She said that her family had to pay for protection. The woman had become infatuated with her daughter and had climbed a lattice on a back porch and entered her daughter's second-story window.

My suspicions were confirmed, and I rejected her gifts from jewelry to crisp heads of lettuce. I knew the risk I was taking. By means honorable and dishonorable she had become the confidante of the District Attorney himself. Trouble was inevitable. One of us would win, and I was not sure which one it would be.

One day a timid little secretary whom I had not suspected of being my friend came to me and said she was going home early and would leave her desk unlocked. At the risk of her position she advised me to read the interview she had transcribed and left in her bottom drawer. It contained the most scandalous accusations against me.

I waited for morning. I was summoned to the head office and confronted with the report. The District Attorney asked me if I had said anything against the woman's reputation. I was aflame with righteous indignation. I replied that I had said nothing against her but that I was now prepared to call her a she-Judas and a sex pervert. The District Attorney was shocked into silence. Finally I asked, "Don't you really know what she is?" The District Attorney turned to the man whom he had called in to witness my discomfort and said, "Do you know what Mrs. Campbell means?" The man replied, "I do and everyone in the office knows it but you." The color drained from his face. He said, "My God, she is a friend of my wife's!" The lady was immediately discharged. The last I heard of her she was one of the matrons in the city jail. I never pursue my enemies.

I shall call the second powerful woman Beatrice, which was not her name. Her husband is still alive and is my friend, and I do not wish to embarrass him, although she never hesitated to do so. She was once known as Queen Beatrice, and like all queens she did some good. She helped to elect a fairly good mayor, and, aided by the Federal Communications Commission, she freed the city of an unscrupulous minister who was misusing the radio.

She had one fault. The lies she told sounded like the truth, and the truths she told sounded like lies. She confused her friends and enemies alike and thereby endangered her position.

I had taught her husband in law school, and I was fond of him, so one day I went to his office with an impressive list of her falsehoods. I warned him that she would ruin them both if she didn't mend her ways. He told me he knew the danger, but not to worry—she was about to go home and raise a family. Instead she went to jail for two years. Her crime was just short of a felony. I think it involved bribery.

She had accumulated enough enemies to overthrow her. I had a qualified respect for the woman and had advised her to retire to a quiet life until the storm blew over. She replied as she did on every occasion when her power was questioned, "I am not afraid. I will hang them on the line." This time her line broke.

I was having luncheon one day with William Bonelli. He asked me what I thought of Queen Beatrice. I gave the answer that the little Sunday-school boy gave when he was asked what he thought of Judas—"Well, she never done nothing to me." Neither of us knew that at that very hour she was dying on a stranger's lawn in Long Beach. When she left the jail she had no desire to live, and she drank herself to death as expeditiously as she had once ruled Los Angeles.

The last of the three women was the most intelligent woman I have ever known. My wits were no match for hers, and the uneven struggle lasted for thirty years.

She was graduated from college summa cum laude at the age of seventeen and married a well-known philosopher, by whom she had two sons. She deserted him for one of his blind pupils.

I first became acquainted with her when my husband retained her as publicity agent for the Bar Association, of which he was president. One could never tell whether she was pursuing you or your husband. She was a Potiphar's wife with a large collection of coats. Wives came to me in tears. All I could say to comfort them was that many lawyers' wives were having the same problem.

She intimidated my maid. When I came home from the theater I would find her asleep on the davenport. She searched my wastebaskets. What does one find of value in a wastebasket? She crowded me off the highway at night when I went riding with my children. She sent me calla lilies. She alternated between vicious acts and unscrupulous kindness. She started a movement to make me president of the Friday Morning Club. When I told her that I absolutely refused to run, she attended the club week after week and sat in front of me watching my every move in a small hand mirror. I was defenseless.

She was not invited when we entertained Sir William and Lady Holdsworth at the ranch. So she sat on top of the hill to glare at the guests as they went by. That night at a banquet given in honor of the Holdsworths she stood in the lobby outside the dining room and wept. When she was asked for the cause of her tears she said that Kemper Campbell had refused her a seat in the dining room. Later, at a trial, she admitted that this was not true.

One afternoon when I was teaching at the university, I saw her coming up the aisle. She was a striking woman, and she commanded the attention of the class. When she reached my desk she said in a voice that all could hear, "I shall never give up until I am accepted socially in your home." I assured her that that would never be. The students gathered around me, and I left my car in the parking lot and went home with two of them for protection.

She supported herself with various activities. One election year when judges were faced with opposition, she went to each candidate and said that for the sum of one hundred dollars a month she would see that they were frequently mentioned in the newspapers. If they did not employ her, she warned them, they would get no free publicity. She was in a position to make good her threat. She signed up eleven judges. That was eleven hundred dollars a month—a small fortune in those days.

Mr. Campbell exposed her, and she sued him for libel. The jury returned late at night and awarded her the sum of one dollar. She was obliged to pay the costs of suit, which amounted to twenty-five hundred dollars. The case was tried before a judge from a mountain district. The local judges feared her and disqualified themselves one by one.

I shall never forget the strange solemn judge, who looked like Midwestern Gothic. When he awarded costs to Mr. Campbell he turned to her and said very slowly, "you are a very . . . intelligent woman. Your talents . . . should be put to better use."

In time distance came between us. I retired from the practice of law and moved a hundred miles away. I saw her once more in Carmel at a breakfast given by the Queen's Bench. She took me by surprise, and for the first and last time I shook hands with her.

She was murdered in 1959. It must have been the work of a friend, for her little dog welcomed the man, glad of his company while he waited for her return.

The shot came from her bedroom as she went into the bathroom across the hall. I was in London at the time and therefore not implicated. No serious effort was made to apprehend the criminal. A general sigh of relief went up from the members of the local bar. Her influence died with her.

Platonic Love

Years ago I attended one of Emma Goldman's lectures. Old Senator Works was in the audience. He was a handsome man with glowing white hair. In the course of her lecture Emma said, speaking of old maids, "How I hate them in all their stale virginity!" Senator Works rose from the front row and with great deliberation walked slowly down the aisle, using his cane at each step with telling emphasis. It was an eloquent defense of unmarried women. At the time, I happened to be one.

There have always been neighboring ranches where guests were welcome without benefit of clergy, and my friends made sport of the guidelines on our ranch. Louis Calhern was one of the worst offenders. He always pretended to other guests that he could outwit me. Perhaps he did, but I never found him out.

In the old days we heated the rooms with fireplaces, and little Mexican maids went around in the morning and lighted the fires before the guests were up. One morning a frightened maid came to me. While she was lighting the fire in Mr. Calhern's room he turned over and said, "Here, honey, is your five dollars. Oh, pardon me, I thought I was at —— [naming a ranch nearby]. Don't tell Mrs. Campbell," which was exactly what he intended her to do.

Perhaps age and experience have made me more tolerant or at least less vigorous in the cause of morality.

The Incas had a strange law. Infidelity was a capital

offense until a man or woman reached sixty. Then they were given their freedom. Time had lowered their biological overhead below the danger point.

I have always maintained that there was no such thing as Platonic love. In my opinion it was neither Platonic nor love and had no place in society. But a strange thing occurred near here last spring which compelled me to change my mind. A hippopotamus wandered away from a small circus and could not be persuaded to return. At last the trainer brought a young elephant to the bay where the hippopotamus was drinking. They had been fast friends. The hippopotamus came ashore and went home with the elephant. Surely that was Platonic love. It could have been nothing else.

A Devoted Son

When I hear a man say, "I owe everything to my mother," I take care. He will be a timid friend and an exacting husband.

Once a minister came to our town to marry a very beautiful girl. I thought she was the most beautiful girl in Sheridan. The Sunday after the wedding he was asked to preach in the village church. During the sermon he said that his mother was the best woman in the world and that his wife was the next best. I was only ten years old, but I knew something was wrong with that sermon. He turned out to be a cruel man. The girl was thin and pale when her parents brought her home, and the church unfrocked the man.

Later in college a close friend of mine was engaged to a good-looking boy in our class. One day the boy told her that all he had he owed to his mother. My friend said she would not marry a man who had nothing of his own. She told him to come back again when he was out of debt and she would talk marriage. That was the end of the romance.

Not long ago the man killed himself by jumping from the top of the Security Bank Building. My friend said he had probably forgotten to tell his mother he would be home late for dinner.

There are few things more pathetic than a grown man who is afraid to disobey his mother.

The Perfect Answer

I have always been amused by the story of the man who went home to his wife and with tears in his eyes confided to her that his secretary didn't understand him.

Years ago I was a young wife married to a very handsome husband. I called at his office when I was not expected. It was after five o'clock, and I opened the door to his private room to find his secretary sitting on his lap. Looking back over her long and faithful service, I think now that she jolly well earned the right to sit on his lap a time or two. But I was young, and this was my first experience with a rival.

I closed the door without saying a word and started walking the street, not caring where I was going. A few blocks away I came to the emergency hospital, just in time to see them carry a little blond-headed boy through the door on a stretcher. I was close to him, very close, and I could see that he was badly injured. I thought of my own child, and I forgot my trouble and gave thanks that he was safely asleep in bed. I turned about, found my car and drove home.

That night I told my husband what had happened, and I said, "I forgot my trouble. It wasn't a tragedy."

Then my husband said the kindest thing. He said, "Honey, you don't love me as much as I love you. If I had found you sitting on another man's lap, I would have thought it was a terrible tragedy."

What a wise man he was!

A Valid Reason

Young women usually marry for one reason, but mature women marry for a variety of reasons—loneliness, boredom, financial security, social standing.

Not long ago a woman I know married for a reason new to me. "My husband has emphysema," she explained. "My first husband died of emphysema, and I know what to do for him."

They have my best wishes for a happy marriage.

❈ ❈ ❈

A Golden Wedding

A Golden Wedding

She said she came to the ranch to get away from her husband. She said if he followed her she would go to the hospital. She has Medicare. She talked very freely about her married life. He had built them a house before they were married. When he brought his first month's pay home he gave her ten dollars and said, "If you need any more let me know." "You put your pay in that drawer, all of it, and I will take what I need," she replied.

Once she went to Florida to get away from him. "If you follow me," she warned, "I will go farther, and you won't know where to look."

When she returned he had an Easter lily on the table as a welcome home. "It was the first Easter lily I ever had," she told me, "but I walked right by the table without saying a word."

She invited one of her grandsons to come with her to the ranch, where he could swim and ride horseback. "I don't know why they never accept my invitations," she sighed. Perhaps they love their grandfather best.

She and her husband will celebrate their golden wedding anniversary the fifth of September. Her sister is coming from Australia for the happy occasion.

The Vacant Chair

I was not invited to the party. It was given in Laguna Beach, some distance from where I live. But a mutual friend told me about it.

The hostess was famous for her parties, and she seldom if ever overlooked an important occasion. It occurred to her that if his first wife had lived her husband would have been marrried to her for fifty years on the sixth of August. She thought about this and decided that it was foolish to ignore the date simply because one of the contracting parties was deceased.

She surprised her husband by inviting a host of friends to celebrate the anniversary with him.

My friend said that the husband was strangely pensive during the evening, but that the party was a huge success. It was one of the best parties our friend had ever given.

Worn Smooth by Time

I have known this husband and wife for over thirty years. I still do not understand them.

Not long ago the husband came to the ranch alone. I asked him where he had left his wife. He said that she had seen an article in a recent magazine which advised a wife to inquire about her husband's business in case the husband died first. The wife promptly followed the author's advice and suggested that he tell her what they owned and where she would find all the important papers in case of his death.

"I shall outlive you," he said, and he packed his indignation with his toilet articles and came to spend the weekend with me. He would reveal nothing to his wife. He said it was enough that he supported her.

I was not disturbed. I knew the marriage would weather this storm as it had weathered so many others.

Later on they came to the ranch together, and the husband became very ill. He was taken to the local hospital in a critical condition. Every morning the wife called the hospital and left the phone weeping.

At last I said to her, "I cannot understand you. In the thirty years that I have known you I have never heard you or your husband give each other a kind word."

"I suppose that is so," she answered. "But I love him, and I couldn't live without him." And she continued to weep. I believed her. She did love him. Her tears were genuine.

"I have concluded," I said, "that you have developed a strange way of life. I think you wake up in the morning trying to see which one can say the meanest thing first."

"Well," she replied, "it is not quite as bad as that. He usually wins the competition." I doubt it.

This marriage will survive while many a husband and wife who "have never had a single quarrel" will long since have been divorced.

Not Recommended

I am frequently consulted about how to spend the leisure years with a retired husband. These are the years—the last of life for which the first was planned. But if they are to be enjoyed some ground rules should be observed.

I know a devoted wife who had a nervous breakdown because her husband stayed home and damned the government every waking hour. Now, I offer my own criticism about the government, but it occupies a minimum of my time. Even prayer can be overdone.

There are many pleasures left for older men and women —some pleasures are even enhanced by age—but having a determined sweetheart is not one of them. This last spring I had to lock my bedroom door for the first time. After the guest was asked to leave he wrote and apologized. He said it was a medicine the doctor gave him. I suspect there are other eighty-five-year-old men who would like the doctor's name.

Married Too Long

It was soon after the First World War, long before charity became a way of life, that I first encountered an ancient wife who did not know what to do with an equally ancient husband. Her church asked me to apply for aid for them.

It was difficult first to prove their ages and then to prove their need. I consulted the census reports in Washington for their ages, and their neighbors assured me they were worthy of help.

They owned their own home, and the husband had a very small Spanish-American War pension. I was pleased when the county agreed to give them an added seventy-five dollars a month. That was so long ago that a man and his wife with a home of their own could come close to living on that amount.

I had devoted much time and some money to this request, and I was expecting gratitude as my only reward. I was disappointed. The wife came to my office looking more downhearted than ever.

"Aren't you happy about the pension?" I asked. She hesitated and then said, "I'ze disappointed. I'ze lived with that old man for fifty years 'n' more. I thought this pension might be a ways to get shet of him. Now it's for us both."

I have heard that story more than once since then—not in those words but with the same deep desire. It's the old complaint, "I married him for better or for worse, but not for lunch."

The number of these forlorn couples increases with the new class of men and women who retire early and have nothing to do but "reside." In some cases there is no necessity for economy, and therefore another common interest is removed. A Darby-and-Joan relationship has a limited appeal after a few years.

The reasons given range from delayed infidelty and unnecessary thrift to trifles like wet underwear in the bathroom or eating apples in bed. There must be some solution for so universal a problem. It is very sad when two people decide to live apart on common memories. Surely there are rules by which one can live with a hapless bore.

One wife solved her problem by moving every year or even oftener. When they moved from the ranch her husband told me that they had moved twenty times in sixteen years. Well, there is precedent for this method. Beethoven moved sixty-nine times. It is expensive, but in the above case it was worth the expense. The couple lived together until the husband died.

Over the years I have compiled a few helpful hints for troubled husbands and wives. I think money spent on a psychiatrist could be better spent on a new wall-to-wall carpet. That always presents a new outlook on life. I have known fresh homemade bread to change the atmosphere of a day that started out to be tiresome. A new bathroom of one's own is a sheer delight. And one husband who was under deep suspicion worked for days to plant a spice garden for his wife. Who could resist such devotion? Within limits an occasional question about the health of one or the other can do no harm.

My aunt married a man who had fallen on the ship which brought him to America. It injured his elbow, and he never fully recovered. When my aunt felt a cool wind blowing she always asked, "Edward, how is your elbow this morning?" It was just as effective as saying, "I love you," and less embarrassing.

Sure the height of felicity
Lies in simplicity.

Breakfast

I hesitate to give advice about breakfasts together. Breakfasts affect people in various ways. There are members of my own family who must first have a cup of coffee before they can be greeted with safety. Other members are like me: they arise in the morning grateful to be alive and meet the day with restrained joy. There is a saying in our family at breakfast, "If you want two eggs grunt twice."

When two people have retired and are striving to live together in relative peace twenty-four hours a day, breakfast presents a problem. One may be an early riser, the other a late sleeper. In this case breakfast is hardly the best place to begin the day. Certainly with leisure both husband and wife should choose the time suited to them even if it means eating breakfast alone. Some men and women prefer to be alone part of the time.

Phyllis McGinley in her book *Sixpence in Her Shoe* tells how she nearly wrecked her marriage in the beginning because she insisted on rising early in the morning and preparing her husband's breakfast before he went to work. Eventually she came to believe him when he said he preferred to get his own breakfast and read the morning paper in solitude.

I know one mother who lost a priceless daughter-in-law because she said, "I wish you wouldn't get up to cook Bob's breakfast. It is the only time Bob and I have alone together." The replacement slept late, but the mother regretted the exchange as long as she lived.

While breakfast is not the best time for a family conference, an occasional family breakfast can be a happy time. Pains should be taken to prepare something special—cream waffles with Vermont maple syrup, popovers with English marmalade, or Canadian herring with hot biscuits. Such feasts open the gates of the day to gracious living.

If You Mean Yes

The doctor and his wife have just left and I am glad. In many ways I enjoy them, but in a short time I grow tired of the way he treats his wife. On this last occasion I told him so. Disrespect of either husband or wife for the other makes conversation difficult; it is like the smell of gas—hard to ignore.

The doctor's defense was that a long time ago, before they were married, his wife had broken their engagement because her family thought he was not good enough for her. He had never been able to forgive her. I said I thought it was foolish that after forty years of being married to her he should still insist on proving that her family was right.

Another doctor once came to my office to ask me to help him get a divorce. I loved both him and his wife, and I declined to represent him. "Why do you want to divorce Cecelia?" I asked. "You will look a long time before you find a better wife." He replied that he had never loved her.

After starting for the elevator, he returned. "I will tell you the truth," he said. "She broke our engagement a month before we were to be married. I guess I have never forgiven her. It was a blow to my pride which I cannot forget."

Another attorney represented him. They have both remarried, and in my opinion she has a better husband and he has an inferior wife. I suspect she said yes the first time her second husband asked her to marry him—perhaps before.

I do not justify these narrow-minded husbands, but I do think that if you intend to marry a man, if your mind is quite made up with no thought of refusing him, it is just as well to say yes the first time you are asked. My husband would never have asked me a second time, and I had no intention of jeopardizing my one opportunity.

If you are invited to a party you do not say no, hoping to increase your self-esteem by being invited the second time. When you work hard for an appointment and it is offered to you, you do not hesitate—not if you are wise.

It is dangerous to humiliate the man you love. Ella Wheeler Wilcox, a favorite poet of my mother's, wrote a poem which I cannot quote and which I cannot find in any anthology. But I do remember she said that when she had humbled a man and he had accepted her terms she found "Alas, I had killed the man I loved."

Forty years ago I had a close friend. She was a beautiful girl with flaming red hair. She was able to go to Wellesley although her family were Illinois farmers. While she was in college, she fell in love with a boy who was a student at M.I.T. After they were both graduated he came to visit her. One day as they were walking in the woods she climbed up and sat on a gate. She wore a sunbonnet. Somehow the sunbonnet is associated in my mind with what happened.

While he stood beside her the boy asked her to marry

A GOLDEN WEDDING

him. "Oh, this is no place to propose," she replied. "Wait until I am dressed for the occasion."

He did not mention the subject again. He left the next day and she was never married.

❊ ❊ ❊

Bold Changes in Education

Bold Changes in Education

California colleges are offering amazing opportunities. They are expanding their courses of study at a rapid rate. There are classes in modeling, hair styling, jewelry design, dancing of various kinds, and even knitting.

We have a friend who is teaching at the University of California at Davis; that is, he teaches two hours a week. The rest of the time he is experimenting with wines. I read in the paper that his wine-testing class was very popular.

In the same daily paper a few weeks later I saw that two doctors from the University at Los Angeles had collaborated on a study of the writings on bathroom walls. They were offended because they were not allowed to survey the bathrooms in the city schools. They are both highly paid professors, and their conclusions should be very valuable—that is, to people who are ambitious to write on bathroom walls.

I called to tell them that I was working on a new manuscript and that I planned to include a clinical report on their clinical report. It was only fair to afford them an opportunity to comment before I completed my study on their study. I said that I assumed this was an interest developed in boyhood and, like Thoreau, John Burroughs, and Dudley Lunt, they had now made a life work of what was once only a pleasure. They both denied it.

They sent me copies of their report. I did not find it interesting—not even interesting enough to show to my friends. But then I am a poor judge of pornography. I did not find the pictures on the walls of Pompeii to my liking.

It may be these two doctors plan to offer a course in graffiti at the university. The class would no doubt be popular.

Right Over Right

The other day I saw a young college student, the son of a friend, walking down the village street. He wore a beard. In a place like San Francisco it might not have embarrassed his parents, but Victorville is a small town, and I knew his parents were ashamed of him. They had paid for his first year in college and they were not happy to settle for a beard. I wondered whether they would send him back to college for a second year.

When I met him downtown I said to him, "Earl, some people pay to hear me talk. I will give you five dollars if you will listen to a lecture on beards." He agreed to come to my home. I let him do most of the talking.

RIGHT OVER RIGHT

He gave all the valid reasons for wearing a beard—it was common in former times, it was neither immoral, illegal nor fattening, appearance did not make the man (this I accepted with reservations). He had a legal right to wear a beard; it was a question of personal freedom.

After he had finished I said, "Let us approach the subject by the Socratic method. Does your beard make your family unhappy?" He had to admit that as a fact it did. "Are you proud of your family?" The answer was yes. "Your family have been very good to you. It was not easy for them to send you to college. Have they earned the right to be proud of you?"

I did not wait for him to answer. "The wisest friend I ever had once said to me, 'The decision of right over wrong is an easy decision to make. It's the decision of right over right that is difficult. That decision causes most of the trouble. It is hard to decide between two rights.'

"One of the most important things in life to me—sometimes, I think, as great as or greater than love—is my family's pride in me. No amount of flattery from others can begin to compensate me for the loss of that pride. When my son was twelve years old I found him in his room crying. 'What on earth are you crying about?' I asked in alarm. 'I am crying because you have no stockings on,' he replied. 'You are going to be just like other women.' It was hot summer weather. Most of my guests did not wear stockings. There was nothing immodest about not wearing stockings, and, besides, it was during the depression and stockings were expensive. I had the legal and moral right to go without stockings, but I have never gone without stockings from that day to this. I had to decide between my right to go without stockings and his right to be proud of me. Did I make the right decision?"

The interview ended without comment, but I noticed later that the boy went back to college without a beard.

Just in Time

Yesterday was Valentine's Day. I received two valentines—one from my granddaughter and one from a little Jewish girl who was one of my pupils when I taught the fifth grade more than sixty years ago. Her name is Lily Shick, and I haven't seen her in all those years. On the bottom of the valentine Lily wrote, "To my dear teacher with love, Lily."

I was told that Lily grew up, taught school, married, was divorced and went back to teaching, but to me she is still a little girl with brown curls and bright brown eyes.

I am glad I stopped teaching while I still enjoyed children. It was just in time. Five years in the fifth grade is quite enough. I pity teachers who have to go on and on and on in the classroom after they are tired of children.

There has been a great change in education. Sixty years ago children were strictly disciplined and no teacher was afraid to exercise authority. Now teachers are taught to obey—obey the superintendent, obey the principal, obey the supervisors and the inspectors and the men who man the curriculum and, last of all, the textbook committee of the State Board of Education.

When I was a teacher we had leisure and less money. Now teachers have more money and no leisure.

Of late educators have been holding seminars at the

ranch where teachers are taught to teach. I have listened in on some of these occasions. The silence is dismal—something like a lecture being given in a penitentiary.

I saw the new book of instructions that has just been issued. It is longer than the Bible and apparently equally important.

Ashamed of America

My granddaughter graduated from Pomona yesterday. I attended the commencement exercises. The graduate who was selected to speak for the class was very bitter about America—all we have done and all we stand for. I have never heard such an arraignment against us either at home or abroad. No Russian diplomat was ever more harsh in his criticism. The speaker recalled every shady act in our history from our treatment of the American Indian down to Resurrection City.

I doubt whether it ever occurred to him that because this country stood for basic human rights, it was his privilege to bring down his curses on it without fear.

I wish I knew what this boy wanted. He didn't really say. If I knew what his goals were and by what specific means he hoped to achieve them, I might help him. But I will never join him in spraying America with my venom.

Perhaps he is like my mother. She used to say, "I want a change even if it is for the worse."

There is a wise Persian saying: "If you do not know where you are going, any road will get you there."

❊ ❊ ❊

Every Home Needs a Grandfather

Every Home Needs a Grandfather

I wonder if one reason for the lack of communication between the present generation and their parents is that there is no longer a grandmother or a grandfather in the house. Every home needs one or the other. It would help to prevent juvenile delinquency. But grandparents have been put in homes for the aged to make way for rumpus rooms.

It is easier for a grandparent to understand a child than it is for most parents.

My younger son once wrote about his grandfather, "He felt that a wheelbarrow was not serving a useful purpose unless it was loaded with dirt going in one direction and with kids coming back. He had a pocketknife for making willow whistles and quill guns. He had hazel eyes for laughing, a large lap to which we could retreat from fear real and imagined, and loving arms within which we were always folded and secure."

I remember once when my father sat rocking my older son in his lap. Kemper Junior was crying—not making a great noise, but sobbing with the rhythm of the rocker.

My mother said, "Grandpa, why do you let him go on crying? You know he has nothing to cry for."

My father answered, "But he wants to cry. I won't always be here. I want him to get all his crying done while I am with him."

Let's Be Honest

Only grandparents really enjoy children, and small wonder. They are an omnipresent nuisance. Dozens of parents with children visit me each year. I am not deceived. The mystery is that people keep on having them.

I remember once when an electrical engineer came to spend a few days on the ranch. He had two small sons with whom he was not well pleased. He was a Yorkshire man, and Yorkshire men are hard to please in any event. These two boys were timid and pale-faced. The engineer wanted robust sons afraid of nothing. He had seen American boys that answered that description.

The first morning, he put one of them on a horse and rode away, leaving him far behind. My daughter rescued the boy. Having failed once, the father sat by the swimming pool until the other son struggled to the edge of the pool, whereupon he pushed him back into the deep water. This time a guest rescued the boy.

At luncheon I said to the father, "I don't blame you for wanting to get rid of these boys. Children are a nuisance, and it will be no better as they grow older. Your mistake is that you are attempting it before too many witnesses. You are in danger of ending up in jail. Now, if you will come to me after lunch I will tell you of ten ways to solve your problem without getting caught."

A final divorce relieved the boys of their father's tyranny and probably saved their lives.

Obedience

I never taught my children to think that I was infallible. I did not want our relationship to be built on a falsehood. I seldom asked their father to support me in a decision. He and I sometimes disagreed on questions of policy. Why assume that I was right just because the children were involved?

It was far better that the children should believe that I wanted to be fair rather than omnipotent. For that reason I encouraged them to appeal to their father if they thought I was wrong. He was often consulted on important problems. The graver the problem, the wiser his advice. The converse was also true.

Mr. Campbell commanded their respect and conformance. He did not belittle himself by fuming and threatening. One sentence, final as a telegram, seldom failed where threats of punishment might go unheeded. "Now that I have expressed my opinion you can do as you please," he would say and emphasize the words by firmly closing the door.

Once when Joe was five years old he wanted very much to visit his grandfather, who had been convalescing in a hospital and was expected home that evening. It grew late and Mr. Campbell said it was time we were both in bed. Joe looked so forlorn that I relented. I was working in the office during the day and had few chances to do him a favor. Joe was eager to see his grandfather and the ambulance. Mr. Campbell went to bed, and we waited until we heard the siren.

In order to reach his grandfather's house we had to cross a busy boulevard. We got as far as the boulevard, and Joe hesitated. He said he was sleepy and suggested that we postpone our visit until morning.

While he was preparing for bed he asked me to tell him about Jimmy Smith. Jimmy Smith had gone to Los Angeles with his mother and had been killed while crossing the street.

"Didn't Jimmy Smith's mother take him to Los Angeles when his father told her not to?" he asked. Now I knew the truth. Joe was afraid to cross the street with me against his father's advice.

❁

Uncertainty

I saw in the paper the other day that little blue Alice Brisbane was engaged to be married.

For years the Brisbanes lived near us. True, they lived twenty miles away, but that made them neighbors on a desert which was sparsely settled. We spent many happy Sunday afternoons together.

The Brisbanes were polite to each other in a gentle way, and the children conformed easily to their father's wishes. It made their guests comfortable, like a warm fire or good music.

The article in the paper reminded me of a day when we were visiting the Brisbanes. The Sacramento Chamber of Commerce had given Mr. Brisbane a chair as big as the old lady's shoe. All the children were playing in the shoe except little Alice.

Mr. Brisbane said, "Alice, why don't you play with the other children?"

Alice replied, "I am afraid you will punish me."

Mr. Brisbane looked hurt. "Alice," he said sadly, "when did Father ever punish you?"

"Oh, you never have," she replied cheerfully. "But you might start any time."

Perhaps this feeling of not knowing quite when parental patience will be exhausted keeps children within bounds. Life with parents always has an element of uncertainty.

Keep Them Busy

The idle are not wholly useless. They invent parlor games and reducing salads, and they stimulate each other to serve in harmless reforms.

Children do not enjoy being idle. It is natural for them to

work, but I would view with alarm a child who at proper intervals, guided by some sure instinct, emptied the garbage pail, solemnly carried in the wood and mowed the lawn. Drudgery is a shiftless habit, like poverty, and once acquired is seldom overcome. It is the result of the inability to plan one's work, as poverty is so often the result of an aimless life.

Work should never be confused with money. All through the depression people talked about being out of work. They meant they were out of money. There is always plenty of work for everyone.

Seldom is work so urgent that it justifies waking a child out of sleep. Sleep is a mystery, one of the sweetest mysteries of life, and a sleeping child is a sad and beautiful sight to see. I never waken a sleeping child without reluctance and only in an extreme emergency. Now that my children are grown I remember with pleasure their every idle hour.

A small boy is a handy gadget to have around the house. One spring day Kemper came home from school as bright as a dime. His eyes were black and shiny and his face had a rosy glow, but he was inclined to sit down. I asked him to help a guest with some luggage, and just as he was about to sit down I sent him for some wood. He tried lying down, and I suggested that he drive into town for the afternoon papers and fruit for dinner. When he returned I kept on playing a sprightly little game, and if he showed signs of resting I quickly thought of something to keep him busy. It worried me to see him idle.

At last he said, "Mama, while I'm up why don't I get dinner?"

Alas, by bedtime the poor child was all broken out with measles. I was so repentant I could not sleep that night. I asked Kemper why he had not told me that he was sick. He replied that he was always so tired when he came home from school that he had not really noticed any difference.

I had forgotten that going to school is a day's work in itself, and a hard one at that. If a man works in an office from nine to five, every member of the family is on the reception committee and has some part in making him welcome and comfortable at night. But when a boy goes to school from eight till three and then is shoved around the playing field for two hours after school, everyone in the family is busier than the Democratic Party trying to find him a job when he comes home.

Clothes Make All the Difference

I do not welcome guests, young or old, who are not becomingly dressed. Long hair, bare feet and worn-out shirts get no farther than the stout front door. Poverty is no excuse. One can dress acceptably by watching the rummage sales.

Clothes have a serious influence on character. My husband once asked me why I did not allow our daughter to wear blue jeans, since she lived on the ranch. He pointed out that her friend on a neighboring ranch wore blue jeans all day long. I replied that I could not control her in jeans. The friend has been married five times. Jean is still living with her first husband. She finds variety in other ways.

Last fall I went to a Liberace concert. I enjoyed it very

much. I wore a silver shift, silver shoes and jewelry and a gray crimmer stole.

While I stood outside the door waiting for friends, a woman approached me and asked timidly, "Pardon me, are you Liberace's mother?" The compliment has given me a new dimension.

Grandmothers Are All Alike

It is much too late to advise my children. The time is long past when they could benefit by consulting me. I might as well have my picture painted on the wall. But I have a compulsive urge to protect my grandchildren. And why not? I have been through it all before.

They accept my warnings in various ways. Sometimes they agree and do nothing about it. At other times they remain silent. They seldom argue with me.

I am quite sure that as long as I live I shall continue to give them the benefit of my experience.

I think all grandmothers have the same desire to be helpful. When Ethel Ferrand was sailing on her first trip to Europe her grandmother phoned her long distance to New York. "Ethel," she cautioned, "do be careful about icebergs. You know they are very dangerous."

A Parrot on His Shoulder

Mildred has been spending the weekend with me. I have known her many, many years. I met her very soon after her husband died and left her with a four-year-old son. She was an excellent mother. She worked hard and gave the boy all the things he needed and most of the things he wanted.

Time passed, and Mildred appeared to have no problems with Arthur. At least, she said nothing to me about them. Then one day she came to the ranch alone. She was worried and unhappy. Arthur was nineteen. He had been growing more and more restless and unkind. One day she said to him, "Arthur, I have done the very best I could for you. I have given you everything I could afford. You are very unpleasant, and since we are not happy together you must just get a home of your own."

The boy was astonished, but he pretended to be relieved. "May I take anything with me?" he replied.

"You may take anything you can load on the car," she said.

I remember that he put his mattress on top of the car and it blew off across the windshield of the man in the car behind. Arthur retrieved it in great haste and said, "Excuse me," before the man could say a word.

Arthur was gone three months. They were hard months for Mildred, but she never relented and asked him to come back.

One day she came home to find him sleeping in his own bed. He had tired of his two companions, who emptied the refrigerator and failed to help pay the rent.

He decided to go to college. Mildred was delighted, but her troubles were not over. He attended Pomona College for a year. It was before the day of the hippies. They were called Flower Children then. Arthur grew a beard and went to school in a sweatshirt with a parrot on his shoulder.

After a year Pomona decided his mother was right and suggested he go to another college.

Now, it so happened that his roving days were over. Let mothers of teen-aged boys take heart from this story. Arthur graduated from the University of Southern California. He is a certified public accountant with a wife and two children. They live in a Cape Cod house in Newport Beach.

Mildred told me yesterday, "Arthur is doing very well. He works seven days a week and is what you might call a pillar of society. Of course I am thankful and relieved." Then she smiled. "But he was more interesting with a parrot on his shoulder."

❄ ❄ ❄

Various Ways to Build Character

Various Ways to Build Character

Neither poverty nor wealth can be successfully imitated. Privation is not always sure to build character. Men who by luck and industry have amassed a fortune are inclined to want their children to begin where they began. It seldom works.

I once knew a very wealthy man who wanted all his children to start where he started. I had many an argument with him, but I could never convince him that he was wrong. He started his favorite grandson at the bottom. The boy was not accustomed to being at the bottom. He became discouraged and committed suicide. It broke his grandfather's heart.

One of my clients has a daughter who is going to school in San Francisco. He is well able to pay her way through college, but he refused to send her any money. He told me proudly that she was working and paying her way. "It builds character to be on your own," he boasted. "She will appreciate an education if she works for it."

The last I heard from him he was not so sure. Her lover

had moved in with her to help pay the rent. It was building character, but what sort of character, I wonder.

Self-Reliance

Two distressed parents came to me not long ago for advice. They were reasonably well-to-do and had only one son. After two years of college he decided to go to work. As soon as he found a job his parents began charging him board and room, so he moved into an apartment in Long Beach with a friend who was willing to share all expenses. The parents enjoyed the boy's company, and now they were sad and lonely. "He might even get married," his mother said in alarm.

I asked them why they charged the boy board and room in his own home. Their excuse was that they wanted him to learn self-reliance. Well, perhaps, but there are other ways.

There is the story of the boy who was taught to be self-supporting by drinking cod liver oil. His father gave him a dollar for every bottle he drank and then took the dollar back to buy another bottle of oil for the boy to drink.

Thrift

I admire thrift, and I deplore waste, but I do not think it is wise to make thrift a ruling passion. I learned my lesson when I broke my leg late at night attempting to turn out a forty-watt electric light.

I was startled one day to find the tenant in the apartment next to mine with an oxygen mask over her face. "Are you ill?" I exclaimed. "No, no," she replied. "We had this tank before my husband died. It was already paid for, and it seemed a shame to waste it."

I know a woman who is almost deaf and almost blind and very, very wealthy and equally unhappy. It pains her to expend any money whatsoever without an adequate return. But she does relent at Christmas time. Each year she instructs her companion to get two crisp dollar bills from the bank. On Christmas Eve she attends the Episcopal church and puts the two crisp dollar bills in the collection. Last year she was ill, and so she still has her new bills. I wonder if they will age before next Christmas and have to be traded in for new ones.

Learning to Spend Money

I had luncheon today with four mothers. Someone mentioned the subject of children and money. It is possible to have problems with one and not the other, but usually there is some connection between the two. These mothers were concerned about teaching their children to save money. I felt they should be giving each other advice about teaching children to spend money wisely.

When my older son was five years old he had an allowance of one dollar a week. That was before inflation. His needs were simple and that amount seemed adequate under the circumstances.

One Monday morning he promptly took his dollar down to the sidewalk and divided it among his playmates. My mother was worried. She said I should teach him the value of money. I replied that the dollar was his, and he had a right to do as he pleased with it. My only responsibility was not to give him another dollar for a week. I was not about to lecture a five-year-old boy on the value of money.

Years later we had a maid with a son the age of my younger son. One day I gave him five dollars. He took the scissors and, to my amazement, cut the bill into pieces so small that they were beyond the redemption of the Treasury Department. My timely interference saved him from an angry mother. "But I must teach him the value of money," she protested. He learned the value of money when the other boys spent their five dollars and he had nothing to spend.

A grieving father came to me years ago. His only son had been killed in an accident with a gun. "He would have been a great man," he mourned. "Just try and get a nickel away from him." I can think of more tender virtues to remember about a ten-year-old boy.

I know many mothers who take a large part of their children's money to put in the bank for them. They hope to accumulate five hundred or a thousand dollars by the time the children come of age. I grant that these mothers are neither selfish nor unjust, but what a sad waste of money. Children are young so short a time—so short a time. Think of the pleasure they might have had. Think of the shining dreams unfulfilled. Stale money in the bank is as useless as a setting of duck eggs in the attic. Nothing happens to it.

I am eighty-two years old, but I still long—how I long—for a tricycle.

※

Lasting Happiness

Not one of my children ever asked me for money he did not repay. When Jean at fifteen and Kemper at seventeen left to go to school in Europe, I gave them the money for their return trip, and I knew they would have it when it was time for them to come home. Our financial structure was based on a few simple rules.

1. The money I gave them had to be spent with my approval. With my money went my advice.
2. Money earned by them or received as a gift for a special occasion could be spent as they pleased, however unwisely. (I was impressed by the soldier on leave who had spent all his pay before his time was up. Someone asked him what happened to his money. "Well, I spent some on liquor and some on women and the rest I wasted," he replied.)
3. Large sums, such as inheritances, had to be invested.
4. Money from the house they built, from the horses they owned and rented to others, and from investment dividends was saved for special purposes such as cars, trips or something that would give lasting pleasure.

When Joe was twelve years old we spent the summer in Europe. The two older children were already there, and we met them in London. The trip was a gift to them—made possible by the fee for a long and bitter will contest. I divided the money equally among the three children and myself. When I gave Joe his share I said, "Now, this is not money to save. This is money to be spent for lasting happiness."

When the train stopped in Arizona, Joe left it briefly and returned with a piece of petrified wood the size of a saucer. "What on earth are you doing with that?" I asked in surprise. "Do you intend to carry that all over Europe?"

"Well," he replied, "you said the money was to buy lasting happiness. Nothing lasts longer than petrified wood. My shopping is done. Now I can just enjoy the trip."

And he was right. When we came home he still had a hundred and forty-five dollars.

Time to Be Generous

A few days ago a friend called me over long distance in great distress. Her sixteen-year-old son was missing. She hoped he had come to me. I would gladly have given him shelter, but he had gone north instead of east. I tried to quiet her fears. I said every young boy had run away from home at some time. The experiment had seldom been successful. W. C. Fields never went home after he broke a potato box over his father's head, but most prodigals return in time.

I told her to look behind the chimney. I knew a boy who took blankets and a supply of food up to the roof of his house and hid behind the chimney. His parents searched everywhere without finding him. All was well for the boy until a neighbor borrowed the ladder. The boy was obliged to come down, since there were no sanitary arrangements on the roof except the chimney.

Well, the lost boy is home again and all is well. I asked his mother why he had left, and she said they had confined him to the house for a month. I don't know that I blame the boy.

There comes a time in a boy's life when his parents can no longer play God. And that time is just as a boy turns sixteen, give or take a month or two. There are still ways and means left to parents, but the tactics are different. It's too late to lock him up and feed him on bread and water. Better to put him on the front porch and send for the Salvation Army.

It is difficult to prove to children in their late teens that you care very much about them. They are inclined to doubt your affection. It may take time and money to convince them that they are not just an annoyance like other relatives. This is the time to be generous and to cultivate their friends. It's a great advantage to have a boy's friends say, "I wish I had parents like yours." Then you know you are on the road to success.

One of the wisest fathers I ever knew told me once, "I had quite a shock the other day. I said to Bert, 'Don't do that or I'll—' I looked at him and there were his eyes exactly opposite mine and just as steady. 'Or you'll what?' he asked. 'I won't like it,' I answered lamely, and there the matter rests for all time."

❋ ❋ ❋

Presume Not God to Scan

Presume Not God to Scan

I am convinced that too much religion is not a good thing. The problem is that no one seems to have the secret—how much to love and fear God and still enjoy life. Religion should be like clear water that washes away the bitterness from life, but it should not wash away the pleasure as well.

No one should ask God to explain our misfortunes. It is a foolish question which He never answers, "for He maketh His sun to rise on the evil and on the good, and sendeth rain on the just and on the unjust."

I know a woman who lost both her husband and her infant son in an automobile accident. She became hysterical over religion and thanked God for her sorrow. Shortly afterward she married a man whom, she assured me, God had sent to comfort her. She was wrong. God had nothing to do with it. The man was a fortune hunter, and not a kind fortune hunter at that. My friend is single and sane again. She is willing to live her own life and accept from

God the comfort He offers to all the bereaved and not expect any personal favors from Him.

The parents of a son who had died in an airplane accident came to spend a few days with me. The boy had promised not to go up in the plane with his friend. He broke his promise and was lost. I wondered what I could say to comfort the mother. Finally I said, "I know what you are going through. I lost a son. I can only tell you what others told me. It gets easier to bear every day. I assure you this is true."

She turned to me with that strange light in her eyes which frightens me. "It was never hard," she smiled. "He is closer to me than he ever was. He knows that he did wrong. He has learned his lesson. He will never do it again."

Probably not.

She has taken a dangerous road beyond human comfort or sympathy.

God's ways are incomprehensible. Let them so remain. "Presume not God to scan," said Alexander Pope.

A Simplified Religion

I went to the Episcopal church with my grandchildren on Christmas Eve. Instead of rejoicing with the angels, the priest chose to defend the doctrine of the Virgin Birth. On the way home I detected a feeling of disappointment with the evening service. It gave me the opportunity to tell my grandchildren about my own experience in college.

A SIMPLIFIED RELIGION

"You are a captive audience," I began, "and between here and home I hope to tell you all I want to say on the subject of religion.

"When I was in college, many years ago, I had professors who were engaged in raising doubts in our minds just as your professors are doing today. There was one professor who had an influence over me. His name was Dr. Lewis Terman, and he later became famous as a philosopher. Dr. Terman was really a great man although he was a devoted atheist. He was very sincere in his disbeliefs. He was about thirty years old, and I was in my middle twenties, and we enjoyed each other and had many talks about religion.

"Dr. Terman argued that Joan of Arc was a greater character than Jesus. She made no claim to divinity, and she suffered martyrdom without a martyr's hope. I am grateful to Dr. Terman for many things. I shall never forget when he said, 'If I believed in a God as vengeful as yours, I would get out of this universe at the first opportunity.' He finally convinced me that God was not waiting to punish me for my sins, at least not immediately, nor was He about to reward me for anything I did or said. Thanks to him I lost my harrowing fear of God.

"Then one day I said to him, 'I want to ask you a question. If you stood by an open grave beside parents who had buried an only child and who believed in heaven, would you talk to them as you have talked to me?' He was honest. He said, 'No, I don't think I would.'

"I continued, 'I am no longer going to discuss religion with you. I have little or no interest in the Virgin Birth. I will not argue about the Resurrection. But you must not take from me the humility of the Lord's Prayer, the short and gentle Sermon on the Mount of Olives, Christ's concern for people whom I would shun, the courage of the martyrs and the glorious belief on which they leaned. You must not take from me all the beauty of the Bible—its words of comfort and joy. What blank pages would be left in precious books if you deleted from them all references to religion!'

"Now, children, I want to ask you one or two questions. Would I have been a better grandmother if I had become an atheist? Would your mother have been a better mother if I had raised her to be an atheist? When your uncle died would I have been happier if I had taught him to be an atheist?"

We had reached home. I did not wait for the answers.

As V. Sackville-West once said, "It seems so simply stated thus—what muddles religion are the decorations which man has added to meet his own needs, fears, and longings for comfort and reassurance."

Disbelief

In our church the quarter hour preceding the sermon is always devoted to the children. They stream up the aisles and sit on the steps of the pulpit and listen intently to a story.

One week we had a missionary's son who was born in Africa. He had a delightful accent, was an apt storyteller and told an exciting tale. It was about a native boy.

His father wakened him one morning and told him to

come and work in the field, but, like all little boys, he turned over and went back to sleep. Later he started for the field and met a group of wild pigs. Now, it seems that wild pigs will eat little boys if they are hungry, and these pigs were very hungry.

The little boy climbed a palm tree, but the pigs saw him, and they started to uproot the palm tree.

The little boy was a Christian, and so he prayed, and then he thought of a way to save his life. He scratched his arm on the palm tree, and he let some drops fall on one pig, and the other pigs ate that pig up. He did it again, and they ate the second pig. At last there were only two pigs left, and he dropped some blood on each pig, and they killed each other. The little boy still had blood enough to climb down out of the palm tree and go to the field to work.

I thought it was a wonderful story, and I sat wide-eyed in the back of the church while the children sat wide-eyed in front of the storyteller.

But when I came home and thought about the story, I didn't believe it. I so often have that trouble when I come home from church.

❊

The Beautiful Land

I wake up in the morning and wonder why I am in Mooréa. It was an old whim which had been long forgotten. I once wanted to go to the South Seas. I revived the whim and flew to Tahiti.

All day and night I hear the laughter of these happy

people. They are a beautiful mixed race. I can find nothing to condemn.

I take no pictures when I travel. I enjoy the smells and sounds of a country—the music of the rain as it falls on the grass roof of my room as it is doing now. No camera can record the call of the barred doves that I hear every morning at sunrise. This is a land of magic, but, like Moses, I am too old to leave my desert home for this promised land.

I have seen much of the globe. I have traveled from Greenland to Tahiti and over most of Europe. I like the earth very much. When I am gone I shall have contributed nothing of value, but neither shall I have marred its beauty. And I have enjoyed the people I have met, from the Pope to a Samoan chief.

From my window I see the waves breaking on the coral reef that completely encircles the island. And on the reef in plain view is the steamer that was wrecked less than a month ago.

It reminds me that when I was a child our church bought a ship. It was to be a missionary ship sailing between the islands of Tahiti, Mooréa, Raatea and Pitcairn. It was to bring supplies and doctors and missionaries to the islands, where they were needed. I gave my entire hoard of dimes and nickels and pennies to help buy the ship.

Alas, its tour of duty was short. After less than five years it was lost in a storm with all on board. I resented that tragedy. I felt that if I could help buy the ship, Providence should have kept it afloat. Since then I have never given my entire fortune to any good cause.

Tomorrow I shall fly home. It will take only eight hours. I shall return these two grandsons to their waiting parents, grateful for their company. I have lived again the days of many years ago when I traveled with the nephew who now pilots our plane and his cousin, the son I lost in the war. These grandsons have the same gay humor and love of adventure. Now I know if you have faith and walk hand in hand with life, life will repeat itself.

Living with a Handicap

Not all handicaps are blessings in disguise, but I give praise to those handicapped men and women who meet the inevitable halfway.

I recall a family who often visit us. They have two children—a beautiful daughter in her teens and a younger daughter who is not quite bright. She has winning ways and with uncommon ease makes a friend out of a stranger. It is a pleasure to see how her parents and her older sister cherish her. One day her mother smiled at me as she took her by the hand. "She is such a joy," she said in all sincerity.

Sometimes a grandfather and grandmother bring their teen-aged granddaughter on vacation. She is not mentally equipped to lead a normal life, but I once spent an interesting evening with her. I received as much advice from her as I gave in return. I wish I could imitate her slight lisp. Her mother was an actress. "But," she informed me, "I like my grandparents best. I am good for them," she assured me. "They have more sense. My mother has been married twice. I told her not to marry this last time, but she wouldn't listen to me. Now she knows I was right. It didn't work. I knew it wouldn't. She never listens to me. She is going to marry again. Don't you think two marriages are enough?" I agreed with her.

"I am never going to marry," she continued. "I am going to be a night nurse, not a day nurse, you see, just a night nurse." I am sure she would be welcomed in the long, dark night by any sleepless patient.

I once knew a brilliant young doctor who found out that one of his two sons was retarded. He locked himself alone in a room for twenty-four hours. There he made his peace with life. When he came out he showed no sign of the struggle. From that day on he was a happy father, and he treats both sons with the same kindness and affection.

There are so many handicapped people in this world that someone has said we are all rejects from another planet. A dull planet that.

It was not always so, but handicapped people are treated with great kindness today. When the Chicago World's Fair was officially opened in 1892 my uncle invited my mother to visit it with him. I was six years old, and I assumed the invitation to include me and my younger sister. I was disappointed to learn that we were to be left at the hotel in the charge of a tiny hunchback. I had never seen a hunchback before, and I was frightened. She looked like something out of a book of nursery rhymes. But the family insisted that we could not go to the parade. Thousands of people were expected, and it would be dangerous to take two small children, the older only six and the younger three.

My mother left us in tears, but our sadness was brief.

The little hunchback wiped our tears away, and, taking us each by the hand, she set out for the parade. Everyone made way for us. The streetcar conductor waited for us and found us a place in his crowded car. We advanced to within fifty feet of the line of march.

When the family returned at night they hadn't gotten within a mile of the parade. We had seen the parade, and President Harrison had smiled and waved to the little hunchback with her two small children.

A Christmas Story

My mother's cousin had died in Chico, in northern California. The woman who kept house for him claimed to be his wife and was asking for the entire estate. I had located his stepson and arranged to meet him in Sacramento and drive to Chico.

It is difficult for two strangers to communicate on a long trip in a car. It is easier if there are three strangers instead of two. But I shall never forget that ride. The man painted a picture for me that is still as vivid in my mind as the pictures which have hung on my walls for years.

It was close to Christmas, and just to be friendly I asked him where he would spend the holidays. I don't remember his answer, but in some way it reminded him of a Christmas he had spent in Russia.

"That was one Christmas I shall never forget," he began. "I was in the American expedition that was sent to save

Russia after the First World War. We landed at Archangel and were pulled out just in time to save our lives.

"On Christmas Day we were rolling over the plains of Russia. I had never seen such a monotonous world. The train steamed ahead hour after hour, and there was nothing on the horizon. The land was like a glistening white plate— no trees, no houses, not a living thing, only a straight line where the snow met the blue sky.

"About the middle of the afternoon I looked out the window, and there was a Laplander in a sled driving a reindeer across that trackless snow. The parallel lines made by the runners of his sled were as straight as the flight of an arrow. The world that year was in pretty much of a mess. I was happy to see one man who knew exactly where he was going," he finished.

It was a long time ago. I think the judge decided in my favor, but nothing that happened in the courtroom is as clear to me as that Laplander and his reindeer on their way to some unseen destination.

❊ ❊ ❊

Your Carriage, Madame

Your Carriage, Madame

After my third child was born, my husband said to me one day, "You are going to look and walk exactly like your Aunt Fanny." Now, we all loved Aunt Fanny, but no one wanted to look like her or walk like her. The observation was intended as a kindness. Instead of being offended I decided to do something about it.

I bought a useful book entitled *Your Carriage, Madame*, and I added a record with directions for morning exercises. Thus fortified, I said to my husband, "I am going to take these exercises for six months, and if they do any good I will keep them up. If they do not help, then you will shut up." I was quite as frank as he had been.

We then signed a pact that has committed me to a lifelong series of morning exercises. Before the six months were up, my husband was complimenting me on the improvement the exercises had made.

Then came a day when I was handicapped by acute arthritis. I had a wise doctor. He insisted that I rise from my bed of pain several times a day and straighten up against the wall. There were times when I had to have help to follow his instructions, but I was faithful, as I always am when I am paying a doctor for his advice. He frequently told me that the first day I failed to straighten up would be the last day I would be able to do so. He said if my back was to fuse, he wanted it to fuse in a line similar to Hogarth's line of beauty and not in a triumphal arch.

I remember that it was in the fall of 1940, because my secretary said she would be glad when the elections were over and we could talk about my arthritis *all* the time.

When I see a poor sufferer doubled over with arthritis I am grateful to the doctor who gave no heed to me when I begged to be left in bed.

I finally recovered from arthritis with only minor damage, and I am still as straight as the Washington Monument, although not as imposing.

It Was All a Mistake

We always have a picnic supper in August. The family invite a few friends and we go up to Wrightwood among the pines.

I insist on preparing the supper, which is the same each year. Among other things I make shepherd's pie. Not the ordinary shepherd's pie with a potato crust—no indeed.

I learned how to make this pie in a curious way. A client came to my office to have a guardian appointed for her brother-in-law. I asked what proof she had that he was incompetent, and she told me that she had made him a shepherd's pie, a dish he dearly loved, and he had thrown it into the garbage can without even tasting it. Whereupon we forgot about the brother-in-law to discuss shepherd's pie, and she gave me her recipe. I do not remember what happened to the brother-in-law, but I have been making shepherd's pie ever since.

Besides making the shepherd's pie, I bake apple pie, make potato salad and homemade bread, and take pickles which I have saved from the jar my cousin sends me each Christmas.

Last year we had a happy time until dark. I came home completely exhausted and went quietly to bed. The next morning I achieved a temperature of a hundred and three. I delight in a temperature without pain. I sleep and sleep and when I dream I have all the aces. That was Thursday. Friday the doctor came.

I hated to be interrupted, but he said I had a kidney infection, and he gave me an antibiotic. It was the second antibiotic I had ever taken. I continued to sleep. Sunday I planned to take my usual place in society, when to my amazement an ambulance drew up in front of my door. I later learned that the doctor was afraid the antibiotic wouldn't work. Of course it was sure to work. I am a doctor's delight. Everything works for me. I suppose my family was alarmed because we had lost a beloved cook not long before with a kidney infection.

Whatever the reason for that ambulance, I was indignant. I protested that I did not need a doctor. I needed a lawyer. But it would have taken the National Guard to protect me that morning. A trip to the hospital costs ninety dollars. I pointed out that I could have gone to Chicago for less, and it would have done me more good.

My brother-in-law and sister met me at the entrance to

the hospital with a wheelchair, and I spent most of three days being wheeled from the laboratory to the X-ray room—back and forth.

It was my first "checkup" in ten years. I keep my nervous system in good repair. I seldom watch television, listen to commentators or pay attention to news that is not a week old. I do not smoke, drink, take sleeping pills or use tranquilizers. So I can depend on my nerves to notify me when I am in trouble.

After three days I escaped from the hospital with the help of my cousin, who was chief of staff. He brought me home the back way, over Angeles Crest. I was embarrassed and so were the doctors. They were deflated to find nothing wrong with a woman past eighty.

Salute on the Highway

Many long years ago I came upon two boys throwing stones and broken bottles into the swimming pool. They ran up the hill with taunting cries, "Old lady Campbell can't catch us." They had forgotten that the hill overlooked the village.

I drove up by a back road and parked on the hilltop, where I could see their every move. They darted down alleys and crossed streets, and all the time they knew they were in plain view of the car above them.

At last they grew tired of the game and went home. I followed them. There I was confronted by a new problem.

Their parents were determined to punish them severely. I begged for mercy and said all I wanted was that the boys clean out the pool the next time it was empty.

Yesterday as I was driving down the village street I passed two grown men. They saluted me with uplifted hats. "Old lady Campbell can't catch us," they laughed.

Ambition

I grieve that I am too old to study music. I always intended to take music seriously when I had the leisure, but music is an accomplishment that cannot be acquired in old age. (I long to play Bach. Bach is my favorite composer. I have two friends who got engaged at a Bach concert and of course have lived happily ever since that day.

I have had a spotted career in music. In my youth I had a few lessons on the organ from an old German professor with a Heidelberg scar across his face. He took a deep interest in my progress, and he once told me I had a gift for pumping. When we sold the organ and bought a piano this talent was lost.

But he paid me one other compliment. Our church was holding a convention, and a young woman came down from Chicago to play the organ. My professor was directing the choir, and he was impatient with her. He said, "Get me Miss Hibben. She doesn't always hit the right notes, but she is always in time." This was the zenith of my career.

Later when I was out of the office with small children I

decided to play the saxophone. The saxophone is a very simple instrument and easily mastered. All went well until my third child was born. As a baby he had a deep-seated dislike of the saxophone. The sound of the saxophone frightened him into tears. Fearful of what effect it might have on the future of this child, I stored the saxophone in the attic.

The family and their friends put on an excellent show New Year's Eve. Talent arrives from various parts of the state and the result is truly notable. I usually make a statement on the ranch finances similar to the President's State of the Union message. But one year to my horror my son and daughter insisted that I play the saxophone. They remembered that I had played it when they were children. I made every possible excuse, even to contracting a slight case of pneumonia. I had not played the thing for thirty years and more. I did not even know the scales. I had no reed. The children insisted. Jean bought me the best reed I had ever used and found a man in town who played the saxophone. There was no way out.

The man worked nights repairing trucks. I found him in a garage with all the doors closed. Before he could send for the police, I told him what I had come for. He was smoking a cigarette, and I decided not to let him use my new reed. So I sat down in a chair, and he sat behind me with his arms around me and refreshed my memory while I practiced the scales.

New Year's Eve came, and I played "Poor Butterfly." The audience gave me a standing ovation. It was my last public appearance.

My Only Claim to Fame

Shortly after I returned from my first trip to England, I happened to be at a dinner with the members of the Supreme Court of the state of California. I criticized them for the clothes they wore while sitting on the bench—salt-and-pepper suits, gray suits and, of all the suits I least admired, brown suits. I suggested that if they would dress in judicial robes, as the English judges do, the public would have more respect for them. The English have a high regard for their judges.

Judge Waste was then Chief Justice. He replied, "Do you really think people would approve of our wearing robes, or would they object to it as being undemocratic?"

I replied that I was sure the change would be popular. "Everyone likes ceremony within reason."

In six months the Supreme Court of California were becomingly robed. The robes were handed down from court to court, until today all judges including the municipal judges wear robes. There is scarcely an attorney alive today who can remember when judges appeared in business suits selected by their wives or possibly their secretaries. For this the state of California is indebted to the English.

The English are masters of the art of pageantry. They know the difference between a mob and a parade. If there are parades in heaven they will surely be in the charge of the English.

How to Enjoy the Stock Market

Every woman around eighty, give or take a few years, should have developed some fixed habits which furnish amusement for her friends and relatives. It is their due. Among other peculiarities which cheer my family is my method of investing money. I follow a fixed system without regard to the antics of the market or the state of the nation. I have my own investment business. I hereby give the public the benefit of my experience.

I buy stocks by the alphabet. I select a stock whose name begins with the letter A, and I proceed through the alphabet to Z, and then I begin over again. I never buy any large amount of any one stock. And I buy only certain stocks. The stock must have at least a B rating, must pay at least two and a half per cent on the market price, and must have paid yearly dividends for a period of five years or longer. These rules limit the field. The stocks that are left are safe for a woman of modest means.

This system has many advantages. I like to receive mail, but I do not enjoy answering letters. By investing as I do I am assured of receiving mail six times a year from each corporation in which I hold stock—four dividend checks, one proxy and perhaps two financial statements. that brings the total to about three hundred letters—almost a letter a day—that I am not obliged to answer. I do not feel neglected when the mail is distributed. Where others are receiving wastepaper advertisements I have only serious correspondence.

My son-in-law is in the investment business, and he looks with kindly scorn at my method. His gravest criticism is that "it takes no intelligence." I hope this is true. I try unsuccessfully to impress him with my success. Last year I was hard put to find a stock beginning with the letter Z. Z's are scarce. I finally waived my own rules and bought ten shares of stock that had none of the qualifications I use as guidelines. I paid nine dollars a share. Yesterday I proudly pointed out to my son-in-law that it was quoted on the exchange at ninety-one dollars a share. His only comment was, "Why didn't you buy a hundred shares?"

Another Prairie Chicken

Quite against my will I find myself turning into a vegetarian. I unwittingly refuse fish, fowl and lamb in favor of our abundant fresh vegetables. This preference is not founded on any principle of health or religion, and for that reason it is hard to arrest or correct. I have never approved of vegetarians, from G. B. Shaw to my late brother-in-law. Perhaps that is because I am myself a reformed vegetarian.

For ten years our family ate no meat. Eating meat was not a "test of faith" in our church. One could eat meat and still be a member in good standing. Tithes and offerings from carnivorous communicants were welcome. But a vegetarian diet entitled one to the inner circle of those who were already prepared to subsist on the food that Heaven provides.

Our ten years of wholesome but restricted diet came to a

sudden and unexpected end. My father believed in the active interference of Providence. There was no such word as *coincidence* in his vocabulary. Quite often he spoke of a fortuitous event as "a voice." He lived by this philosophy for over seventy years, and I am persuaded that it is as good a theory as any by which to solve the uncertainties of this life.

One autumn day as my father drove along the country road near our home a large well-fed prairie chicken flew against a telephone wire, broke its neck and fell dead within a few feet of his horse. He brought the chicken home and convinced my mother that it was "a voice"—that our years of semifasting were over.

We are old women now, my two sisters and I, but we still remember that prairie chicken. I have eaten in famous restaurants here and abroad, but no food has ever surpassed that prairie chicken. From that off-ramp away from asceticism we proceeded to chicken tamales and shortly to meat of all kinds.

I regret that I am losing my liking for meat. I can only hope for another prairie chicken.

❊ ❊ ❊

On the Edge of Time

On the Edge of Time

While there are no sensible ways to prepare for death, there are habits that lead to happiness for our declining years.

I think first of books—books that "bear us lands away," books to read together, books to enjoy alone. I can live in a world of books. I could not live in a world without them.

I once visited a friend whose home was near Cambridge, England. He lives in a house that was built the year Saint Joan was burned at the stake. I do not know why I always connect this happy house with that unhappy event. My friend has converted the old buttery into a library. "What new books have you read lately?" I asked him. "None," he replied, "I have a hundred old books I have not had time to reread."

Television is in competition with books. It is a blessing to some of my friends, but not to me.

Then there is music to be shared or to enjoy in solitude. Husband and wife should each have a favorite composer to vary conversation. To disagree over composers is a pleasant pastime. My favorite composer is Bach. I approve of his phrasing—as satisfying as the multiplication table—and I rejoice in his cathedral-like structures of sound.

Travel while you may, preferably by air. I resisted airplanes until I was seventy. Then I realized how little I had to lose. I covered my loss with insurance and took to the air. I entered a new, thrilling dimension. This year I took my two oldest grandsons to Tahiti. What could I possibly do in Tahiti? Nothing at all. But I saw Tahiti through two pairs of youthful eyes lighted with wonder. What if death had found me in Tahiti? It would only have added to my personal significance; almost as dramatic as the old man who died this spring climbing the Angel Trail up from Grand Canyon. That is death with poetry.

The last few years should be spent in a place one can enjoy—in the woods, by the sea, on the side of a mountain. To each of us will come the day when our world is framed by a wide window. I have chosen the desert. As long as I live I shall enjoy the blue and gray of new desert leafage, the geranium red of young scrub, the pink tips of the mountains and their purple depths of shadow. And when I can no longer go to them, the birds will come to me.

In the words of F. Tennyson Jesse, "Let beauty not die for me. May the young moon cradle magic and the old moon image peace, may the wind never fail to blow freedom to my nostrils and the sunlight strike to my heart till I die."

Old People Live Too Long

I agree that old people live too long. As Sir Thomas More said, "The long habit of living indisposeth us for dying." Now that I am among the oldest of the old people I see the problem close at hand.

Age does not give one the right to disrupt the family life of the next generation.

Not long ago a daughter came to a party at the ranch. With her came her mother, who could scarcely see, could not hear and found no pleasure in food. She had followed her daughter day and night for forty years. The mother died last week, but the daughter has only a small share of her own life left to live. She is seventy-four.

Yesterday I attended the funeral of a dear friend. For more than five years before her death she could not leave her mother for a day. The mother refused to have a companion with her. Left alone, she either ran away or planned some other mischief. I saw the mother at the funeral. She looked very well. I did not congratulate her on her hundredth birthday. She should have died long ago and let my friend live.

On the other hand, everyone young or old should have something to live for, something to dream about. Happiness is possible as long as life lasts.

It was a terrible blow to my father when he had a cruel stroke. He had been so young for seventy-five. He had grace and pride. Now all was changed. Even his disposition changed. He became difficult. He had never been difficult before. He slept in the daytime, when the nurse was on duty, and stayed awake all night demanding constant attention.

It broke my heart to think that he had nothing to look forward to. Loving care was not enough. So I said to him, "Papa, from the day we are born there are things we will never do again. Jean will never turn another handspring, I will never skate again, and you will never ride another horse. But one is never too old to be thoughtful of others. You must learn to lie awake during the day and sleep at night when the nurse is gone."

"But I can't sleep at night," he sighed.

"At least you can try. You are never too old to try," I replied. "I will make you a promise. If you will learn to sleep at night, I will take you to the ranch one week each month. I will take you if I have to take you in an ambulance. I will give you a bed next to the window where you can look out over the ranch all day."

He loved the ranch. It was there he had spent his happiest carefree days. His eyes lighted with joy for the first time since his stroke. I kept my promise, and from that day until he died he slept through the night.

Most old people are easily pleased. Families should invent some scheduled attention to make old age less deadly.

I know a very intelligent woman who lives in Pasadena and writes for the *Geographic*. She has never married, but she has lived a good life. Her mother has always lived with her. Her mother is self-contained. She is not a burden to her daughter.

Two years ago the mother was very ill and had to be taken to the hospital in an ambulance. Home again, she talked continually about the ride—she enjoyed the two attendants and she enjoyed watching the traffic make way for them. Finally her daughter arranged to have the ambulance call for her mother once a month, take her for a ride around the city and bring her home again with the siren blowing. The mother has something to look forward to. It is money well spent.

The Coward

Lady Diana Cooper once said, "The long custom of living disciplines one to dying, and great loss makes death less fearful. Besides, before the end what light may shine?"

He left an hour ago, and what a relief it is. A man who is afraid to die is a great nuisance around the house. This man is past eighty, and he should be accustomed to the thought of dying by now, but the older he grows, the faster he runs from death.

The first thing he does when he visits me is to engage a doctor. He is trying to find a doctor who will promise him immortality. His finger is on his pulse a good part of the time, until I find the whole family doing the same thing. The last I saw of him he was driving toward Camarra as fast as the law allows.

I well remember the first time I came face to face with my own death. I was in the office when I suddenly discovered that I had a heart and that something was wrong with it. One of the partners was in the next room. I went to him for comfort. He felt my pulse, and he was as frightened as I was.

I thought of my three small children—of their father's bewilderment, left alone to raise them. Death withdrew, and I did not see his face again for fifty years. When he came again I was not afraid to die; unwilling perhaps, but not afraid.

I remember what W. K. Kellogg once said to me. He had eaten an unreasonable number of persimmons, and they came near to proving fatal. "I was not afraid to die," he said, "but I was ashamed to die."

My son-in-law does not plan to die. He argues like the ancient philosophers that just because the sun came up this morning is not a sure sign that it will rise tomorrow. After the same fashion he argues that just because everyone so far has died is not proof that everyone will die. I think time will prove him wrong, but there are signs in his favor. The average span of life has doubled since I was born, and scientists are bent on replacing worn-out vital parts.

Preoccupation with death went out of vogue long ago. Certainly it is a pity to waste the last happy years of life preparing for death. It is an insult to life. I try to attend some church once a week, but not to prepare for death. No change that I could make would greatly affect me or benefit my family. Like the man who was sentenced to prison for life. When someone exclaimed, "All your life," he replied, "Oh no, only for what is left."

Death has signed no armistice with life. Death, like time, can be neither accepted nor rejected. When Mary, Helen Hayes's daughter, was born, her father, Charles MacArthur, said, "We have given her two gifts—life and death."

"Well, that is how things are in this unsatisfactory world. God give us all a good journey out of it," says Clemence Dane.

By Appointment

The guide asked me if I would like to see an osprey.

"Yes," I answered, "I would like to see an osprey." So he took me to the canyon, and I saw an osprey sitting on her nest.

Mildred asked me if I would like to see a green-backed towhee.

"Yes," I replied, "I would like to see a green-backed towhee." So she took me to Table Mountain, and I saw a green-backed towhee singing on a toyon bush.

The doctor asked me if I would like to see a turnstone.

"Yes," I said, "I would like to see a turnstone." So he took me to the Big Sur, and there I saw a turnstone playing in the waves.

Marion asked me if I would like to see an oyster catcher with ruby-red feet.

"Yes," I said, "I would like to see an oyster catcher with ruby-red feet." So she took me to Montana d'Or Park, and I saw an oyster catcher with ruby-red feet standing on a rock by the sea.

Is it true that "not by appointment does one meet delight"?

Still Remembered

My granddaughter was flying to Denver. Friends and family were gathered around her, waiting for the plane. I noticed a middle-aged woman who was listening to the conversation. It happened that she sat beside Celeste on the plane.

She turned to Celeste and said, "I overheard part of your conversation. Are you related to Kemper Campbell, Jr.? You mentioned the name of the ranch."

"He was my uncle," Celeste replied. "He was killed in the war before I was born."

"I know," the woman replied. "I went to school with him." She looked out the window for a long time. When she turned back to face Celeste she was wiping the tears from her eyes. "I am sorry I asked," she said. "I thought I had forgotten him."

The River Is Safe

The River Is Safe

Life has an admirable habit of meeting its obligations. It may take years, but payment is assured.

In 1927 my husband and I were in Sacramento trying to induce the legislature to raise the judges' salaries from six thousand to nine thousand a year. We met with such success that the momentum has carried on to this day. I think the last legislature raised the amount to twenty-five thousand, and it will doubtless go higher. But that is not the point of this story.

While we were in Sacramento a man came to Kemper and said, "I hear they are taking the Mojave River through the mountains to southern California."

Kemper replied, "That is certainly not true. The Mojave River flows through my ranch. I have valuable water rights along the river, and I have heard nothing about the plan."

The man replied that the subject was before the committee that very evening and that they had already started the bore through the mountain. It was true. Kemper went to the committee meeting and defeated the bill.

THE RIVER IS SAFE

The next day one of the men interested in the plan came to him and said, "Kemper, you are making a mistake. We have set aside four hundred thousand dollars to pay for your water rights."

I shall never forget my husband's reply. There was dignity in his wrath. "There is not enough money in southern California to buy that river," he said. "That river belongs to future generations and to the birds and the animals that have their homes along the river. It runs through what would otherwise be a desert land. Once you kill a river it is dead forever. It will never flow again."

There have been times in the forty years since that day when I have thought of that four hundred thousand dollars. With higher taxes, higher labor costs, floods, dry years, and declining prices, it has been a struggle to maintain the ranch, but I have never once wished we had sold the river. I love anything that flows. Even when times were hardest we consoled ourselves with the thought that we would probably have lost the four hundred thousand in the stock market that bleak October day in 1929.

The state of California has just purchased half the ranch for a state game-and-wildlife refuge. The park will be called the Mojave River Park. The river is safe. It will never be put upon—which has been the fate of the Feather River and the mighty Colorado. It is forever free.

I wish Kemper had lived to see this day. The Mojave River is his living memorial.

Forty Years Have Passed

Now that we are selling half of the ranch for a state park, my mind goes back forty-four years to the time when I first came to Victorville. Mr. Campbell had owned the ranch for six months before I saw it. He bought it for an investment and did not plan to make it our permanent home.

The road to the ranch led through miles of familiar orange groves, then up a narrow canyon and through the mountains to Cajon Pass. It was already late afternoon when we reached the summit. I looked out upon a land that was as strange to me as the veldt or the pampas. The sunlight was like a golden mist over the limitless sand. The distant unwatered hills stood knee-deep in purple shadows. The valley between was covered with curious shrubs and ancient trees.

As we descended from the summit I had a feeling that we were standing still while the trees were moving about us. The wild lilac and the red-limbed manzanita stole in among the junipers. The junipers with their delicate blue berries edged between the strange twisted Joshua trees. The Joshua trees in turn stood apart for creosotes and honey mesquite.

Fifteen miles from the summit we turned off the highway and drove up over a low hill. The last rays of the sun softened the pile of giant rocks that guarded the narrow entrance to the valley that belonged to us. My cousin once said that these rocks were the burdens people dropped as they came over that hill.

The valley was bounded by a range of low-lying hills to the west; a sheer cliff separated it from the mesa on the east. The Mojave River flowed through the ranch from end to end. Willows and alders and cottonwood trees lined its banks. The tender green of the alfalfa fields spread like new paint over the gray tissue of the desert.

It was the quiet hour of the day, when all sounds keep close to the earth. Cows were grazing in the pasture nearest the house, and the horses stood with their heads over the fence of the corral, waiting to be turned out.

I knew at once that our days of searching for a place to live were over. We had come home.

Ignoring the Depression

It was a day to be remembered, that Friday in October. We went to work in the morning feeling secure and came down to lunch to find half our fortune swept away. It was a comfort to go that night to the ranch, where everything remained the same.

The men who lived in the valley took little or no notice of what had happened to the stock market. Some of them had lived along the river for fifty years. Some of them had not even seen Los Angeles. They had never known abundance and they could not lose what they did not have. Nothing in their lives had changed. The cottonwood trees shed their yellow leaves, the quail came down from the mountains, the deer season opened. Between the low hills and the river life went on as usual. No depression can endanger wealth that depends on earth and sun and rain alone.

I accepted their philosophy. We had thought we were rich and now we were poor. We worked harder, and over the weekends I cooked and did the family washing. There was never a time when doing the family washing raised the level of prosperity or was in itself necessary. But doing my own work was an economy I could understand. I was on a level with my neighbors. It gave me a false importance which I enjoyed. It was a substitute for anxiety.

I was not really frightened by hard times. I always regarded Mr. Campbell as a combination of Abelard and the Bank of England. If the Bank of England failed there would always be Mr. Campbell.

Time passed. Our finances improved. The wolf grew tired and left our door.

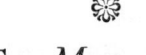

Too Many Cooks

I think it was the poet Thompson who said that civilized man could not live without cooks. At times I was sorely tempted to try. I wonder how many of these women of power and influence took possession of Mr. Thompson's kitchen. There have been days when I hesitated to enter my own kitchen for fear of inciting a riot or a resignation.

There was Susie and her husband. Susie was the cook, and her husband waited on her and did the heavy work.

THE RIVER IS SAFE

The family consisted of Susie and her husband and a monkey. Susie's husband told me the sad story of why they took the monkey to raise. Susie had lost a child at birth, so he said, and he bought her the monkey to keep her company. I insisted that the monkey sleep in a tight shed behind the house.

One night it turned cold suddenly, and the poor monkey's tail froze. The next morning Susie cooked the breakfast, but left before lunch. They had to take the monkey to a warmer climate. I never heard from them again—they did not even ask for unemployment. I felt responsible for what happened to the monkey, but there was never any news of him. It was useless to look in the obituaries; monkeys are not recorded in the column of vital statistics.

Some of our poorest cooks have had good voices, and the kitchen echoed with melody. One Saturday evening all the family went to a neighbor's wedding. We returned later than I had expected, and I was surprised to see a woman dressed in a black evening dress standing in the bow of the piano, singing "The Last Rose of Summer." I did not recognize her until she spoke. "You were gone so long," she explained, "the guests were getting restless." She was our new cook.

I have learned never to engage a cook who has had any previous professional experience. There was the woman who came directly from a restaurant in the village. The first night that she cooked alone we had several friends to dinner. She surprised us by baking the lamb and the ham in the same roaster. It gave each of them a new flavor. She said she could never tell the difference between ham and lamb—"They sound so much alike."

Intelligent cooks can usually do other things as well—

TOO MANY COOKS

like selling real estate, for instance. There was Martha. Cooking was not exciting enough to satisfy Martha. When a new subdivision opened up near us she added selling lots to her other duties. I have seen Martha put lamb chops on the grill, go to the phone, sell a lot in Hesperia and be back at the stove in time to turn the chops. Martha did well until titles became involved and problems arose that even the lawyers could not solve, so she moved to Nevada, where she continues to prosper.

Martha was a good cook, but after she left I learned that she promptly threw all her failures into the garbage can, where they belonged. That is one rule for success—never emphasize your failures.

A cook may be able to combine real estate with cooking, but it's been my experience that no cook can be pastor of a church and do a good job in the kitchen. This cook had Sundays off, and she put a bow in her hair, took her electric guitar, and went to Lucerne Valley to save sinners. Why Lucerne Valley? I never saw a sinner in that quiet little town at the foot of the mountain.

She had other interests besides her church and the kitchen. She built a structure behind the red house in her spare time. I never knew what its purpose was. When it was finished it would safely house a lion. The men were annoyed. They said it was just a road barrier of a strange design.

One day she told me she had a call from the Lord to go to Twenty-nine Palms. I was happy to see her go. Since she left us for a better offer, she could not ask for unemployment.

I was gone the weekend before she left. She brought a Gospel singer from the city and held a revival service in my front room. There were no converts.

The cook I pitied most was Jessie. Her husband had left her, and she was very lonely. Jessie had a big heart, and she was easily persuaded that another woman's husband was in love with her. I saw him very often when he went with Jessie to the market to buy groceries for himself and his wife. I do not remember his name—all I remember is that Jessie called him "Sweety."

I protested when she loaned him the two thouand dollars she had received as a settlement from her husband. I tried to tell her how foolish she was. She went to the window and burst into tears. I could say no more. "Sweety" was the only spot of color in her drab life. There is no one as hopeless as a lonely woman in love—in love with just anybody.

I saw the lightning and waited for the thunder. It came on Labor Day. I welcome all holidays with the exception of Labor Day. It comes at the end of summer, vacations are over, reluctant children are going back to school, and I am worn out. But no other Labor Day compared with that one. We had fifty guests. It began with a quarrel between me and a friend. I was wrong, and we are still friends. Then one of our kindest horses broke his leg in the pasture and had to be shot.

At five-thirty the girls informed us that Jessie had not arrived. The pies were in the refrigerator and the prime rib was in the oven. For all Jessie knows it is still there. My daughter phoned the hospital; she phoned the sheriff's office. At last we looked in her room, where we should have looked in the first place. It was locked and empty, and a husband was missing. I could hardly blame Jessie for snatching at happiness. After all, she had fed him and his wife for months.

Later the husband phoned his wife collect to see if she

was keeping up the payments on the car they were using.

The last I heard of poor Jessie, "Sweety" had deposited her together with her trunk at the side of Sepulveda Boulevard, and there he deserted her. In due time he came home to his wife.

Our troubles with cooks ended ten years ago. At that time we adopted a family of excellent cooks. They are among our most cherished blessings.

Dogs

Every ranch should have a dog. We have had a series of dogs. Some of them have deserved my love and affection. Some of them have been scoundrels and passed on leaving me with no regrets.

The first dog to make the ranch his home was a springer spaniel named Crooner. The director Frank Bacon gave him to the children. But he had lived too long in Hollywood to settle down to domestic life. He left us for long vacations. Once after an absence of several weeks we saw him in the ring at a local rodeo, putting on his own act. When he caught sight of the family in the bleachers he greeted us warmly, intimating that we had deserted him.

He was a continual source of revenue for the little boys in Victorville. I gave them fifty cents every time they brought him home from town. I had to make a rule that I would pay for only one trip a day. It was hard on him to go back and forth all day long. I think it shortened his life. He died young.

After Crooner came Sausage. How do dogs come by such odd names? Sausage had excellent manners. He was polite to strangers but brave if he suspected foul play. He used to sit quietly at Jean's feet with an expression of complete contentment. The day Jean married he wore a white bow and watched the ceremony. He never liked Jean's husband, because after her marriage he was not allowed to sleep in her room.

He grew old and resented children. I could hardly blame him. He was a menace to Jean's nephews. It was a sad day for us all when she took him away. No one mentioned it when she came home alone, but the next day her husband said, "I can never love you as that dog did, but I will eat dog biscuits for a week if it will help."

Our next two dogs were beagles. Beagles happen to be my favorite breed. If a dog howls at night, let it be a mournful sound like the voice of Bugle Ann. Sometimes I like to be sad at night.

One dog was small, alert, and brave. The other was fat, lazy, and stupid, and besides he was a sex pervert. The vet gave him shots, but it did no good. It seldom does. He had one kind act to his credit. He gave his brother a blood transfusion when he was mortally wounded trying to protect the ranch from a mountain lion. But his brother did not live through the night. He heard Jean's voice, wagged his tail and died. I don't remember what became of his lazy brother, and I don't really care. I am glad his mother never saw him after he grew up. He was a cute puppy.

We have two dogs now with whom I find no fault. One belongs to my daughter. He followed her home from the hill one day. I shudder to think what would happen if Jean ever walked through a jungle. All animals follow her home.

DOGS

Waif is the dog's name. He is a large ungainly collie. His carriage is awkward, without bounce or rhythm. He must have had Saint Vitus' dance as a puppy. He unfolds one joint at a time, and even when he is standing up he hesitates before deciding which foot should go first.

But he is my favorite of all the dogs I have known. Quarrels make him nervous. It may be because he has taken so much aspirin for his arthritis. Whenever a member of the family raises his voice and Waif thinks a quarrel is impending he goes from one to another making the most doleful sounds. It is quite impossible to maintain one's anger in his presence. He is a man of peace and has silenced many a dispute. I only wish he would father a long line of peacemakers, but alas, Waif is not a family man.

The other dog now residing on the ranch is a trim, small dog named Boston. I am told she acquired the name because she is the color of baked beans. She is a general favorite with family and guests, but she accepts no responsibility. She spends most of her time riding around the ranch on the heavy equipment. Not long ago she met with a serious accident. Finally the vet said that the only way to save her life was to fly her to Beverly Hills for an operation. She had a ruptured diaphragm, and after the operation she was placed in an oxygen tent and given blood transfusions.

I have to admit that Boston's personality has changed since her operation. She is more aloof and less inclined to be friendly with strangers. One of the tenants who is on her list of friends said the other day, "If that dog tells me about her operation once more, I am not going to let her in the house."

Horses

Horses should write the history of this ranch. They are the permanent residents.

When we bought the ranch more than forty years ago there were at least thirty horses on the ranch—half of them of no possible use. The former owner posed as a rancher from Montana. I think he really came from Montana, but I am sure the state of Montana was relieved when he moved west.

He boasted that he could break a horse in a day. To prove it he drove a beautiful span of matched bays at top speed four miles on a hot July day. He "broke their wind"—that is, he damaged their hearts so that they could never be driven again. Victorville was a border town, and like every border town they loved and respected horses. They ordered the man from Montana out of town at the point of a gun, and he never came back.

We have owned a long line of horses, many of whom I like to remember. There was Bourbon—a beautiful brown horse with a gentle disposition and an even gait. That was thirty years ago and the guests are still asking about Bourbon. Bourbon made trouble between them. There was competition, not always friendly, about who should ride him. I came home one Friday night after a week in the office to find the guests divided into two hostile camps. One lady had said to another lady, "You should not ride Bourbon. You are too heavy." There is no greater insult to a woman's pride. The result was that Bourbon got a week's rest.

So many horses' lives end in tragedy. We once posted a sign which read, "Three of our horses have been killed by careless riders. The next time a rider ruins a horse we reserve the right to shoot the rider instead of the horse."

The river pasture is especially good for polo ponies that need a rest. There is plenty of shade and a river where they can bathe their tired feet. One year we pastured a string of polo ponies belonging to Mr. Havenstright. Two of them were missing when the polo season opened. We looked everywhere for them. The pasture is in the middle of the ranch. They could not have strayed or been stolen. Months later one of the men saw a horse's head emerging from the swamp. Cows will safely cross a swamp where horses will panic and sink deeper and deeper into the quicksand. These horses must have been frightened by something, possibly a mountain lion, or they would never have dared to cross where they were not sure of solid ground. Mountain lions prefer horses to cattle. They will creep through a herd of cattle and come up on a defenseless colt. We lost a registered Arabian colt not a quarter of a mile from the house. The tracks of the mountain lion were conclusive evidence.

Will Rogers retired many of his horses to the ranch. He came to see them very often. He would stand at the gate and whistle and they would recognize him and come to the gate to greet him. Dopey, his favorite, died and was buried here. The children kept his grave clean until the flood of 1938 carried him away, grave and all.

One tragedy the family will never forget. We were at the breakfast table when we heard the whistle of the fast mail train. We knew from the continued blast what was happening. The pasture gate was open and the horses were grazing along the railroad right of way. The tracks were half a mile away. It was terrifying to see the mail train bearing down on the horses, confusing them with whistle and bell. We watched with horror, helpless to turn away from the window. The horses parted to let the train pass—all except Jess, a beautiful palomino. She went racing down the track, her flaxen mane flying like a flag on a sinking ship. The train slowed down, but it could not stop. It passed by and the brave horse was gone.

Jess left a little filly. Perhaps because she was left an orphan she grew up to be an outlaw. She was as beautiful as her mother, but nothing could break her independent spirit. We called her Bad Jess. When I saw her go over backward with one of my sons I told him never to attempt to ride her again. "But, Mother," he protested, "who will break her? The cowboy doesn't dare to ride her. He has children. I don't." I told him I was not risking a ten-thousand-dollar boy on a hundred-dollar horse. We sent Bad Jess to a training school for horses, but they gave up, and she went from there into a career as a wild horse on the rodeo circuit. She was always ambitious. It would have grieved her mother.

Another ambitious mare was sent to us to spend the rest of her life. She had been a famous jumper, and when her owner died she left a trust fund for Nora's support. Nora had only one ambition and that was to jump fences. We were hard put to build a fence high enough to restrain her. Finally we decided that having a colt would give her something to live for and she would forget her past glory.

With the trustees' permission and Nora's consent, we bred her to our stallion, but it did no good. She practically ignored the colt, and he followed her around while she looked for and sometimes found a fence she could jump. She had no apparent desire to leave the ranch. She simply wanted to jump fences.

One spring a moving-picture company made a picture on the ranch. A lovely little palomino named Pal mistook the signals and ran straight into a barbed-wire fence. She was badly cut, and she stayed with us for two months and we became well acquainted. The next Christmas we bought Pal for Jean. She was trained to rear with a rider on her back, to shake hands and to put her front feet on a barrel. When the Arthur Brisbanes lived near us they used to visit us Sunday afternoon, and the children always asked to see Pal perform. One Sunday Pal was nowhere to be found. The children organized a search and rescue party according to Boy Scout directions, and they found her in a round mudhole from which she had no possible way to escape. Pal was no longer a palomino but completely covered with brown mud. Jean stayed up all night with hot food and warm blankets. The visit from the Brisbanes saved Pal's life. By morning she would have died of exhaustion and exposure.

The children learned to ride on a gray horse known as a cradle horse, meaning that she liked children and that children were safe with her. When the children outgrew her we turned her out to pasture. Mr. Campbell believed that all old horses were unhappy. He decided that the old gray was bored with life and would rather be dead. We watched with sorrow while she was loaded into a trailer and left for the fox farm, but before the children had dried their tears she was back in the pasture where she belonged. I never knew how she managed to escape from the trailer and find her way home.

I no longer ride the range. My favorite horse was a large

graceful creature named Felipe. Felipe liked women, me included, but he had no tolerance for men. I was always proud when a man came back after a rough ride to say, "You should not ride that horse. He is too much horse for any woman to handle." While I was recovering from an attack of arthritis Felipe died. I have never loved another horse as I loved Felipe.

I have great sympathy for horses. Such boundless love and affection is spent on dogs and cats and monkeys, and so little in comparison is spent on horses, who do so much more for man. I remember long ago when a farmer was respected not only for the table he set for his family, but also for the way he fed his horses.

Once I was giving a dinner during the holidays and my Aunt Emily, who was the famous cook in the family, offered to help. She lived on a farm two miles out of town. Unfortunately the day turned out to be one of those miserable days of intermittent sleet and snow and gusty wind. At nine o'clock Aunt Emily arrived. Her head was wrapped in a "fascinator" and she wore her husband's overcoat.

"Why, Aunt Emily," I exclaimed, "you didn't walk all the way, did you?"

"I certainly did," she replied. "I wouldn't take a horse out in this weather."

Spring

This has been a rare spring. I have never before seen so many blossoms on the Joshua trees. Every branch is tipped

SPRING

with glistening flowers like bunches of white figs. Have these timeless trees set about to deceive the Park Service and make me regret that I signed the deed?

Plants and animals who live on the desert must make a final adjustment to their surroundings. Those who cannot survive drought, freezing weather, and summer heat are finally eliminated.

There are lilies whose bulbs are buried deep in the ground and yet who know when the rains have fallen and when it is safe to send up their fragrant white blossoms.

There are seeds that lie dormant for years or produce plants only an inch or two above the ground until a wet season comes. Then they will grow knee high like the evening gilia which covers the desert with its lavender flowers.

Trees conserve their moisture for years—waiting to replenish themselves in a year of rain. The Joshua tree was doubtless the first tree to survive on the desert, and it will be the last to perish. It has outlived birds and animals long extinct. It grows slowly, sending out a cautious branch every five or six years. It is very difficult to transplant a Joshua tree, and some say it must be transplanted by the compass, north to north and south to south, if it is to live.

Joshua trees do not take kindly to the attentions of men, and they resent irrigation. Once a doctor who lived with us planted a Cape Verde tower of jewels close to a Joshua tree directly in front of the house. He watered his tower for four years before it bloomed. In September the Joshua tree fell over dead. The doctor cut it into lengths for the fireplace, and from time to time he burned a piece to delight the children. It made a fine display. He left the topmost branch to the last, and in April it blossomed.

Dust

They tell me there are over thirty thousand people living in our valley today. There were perhaps three thousand when we bought the ranch in 1924, and that included our neighbors for twenty miles in each direction.

I wonder if many people with their houses and lawns and shade trees do change the weather. It must have been twenty years ago that we had our last dangerous dust storm.

It came at the end of a dry season. No rains had fallen for months, and clouds drifted from the mountains only to raise false hopes of showers that never came.

The morning dawned hot and still. Not a leaf was stirring. The sunrise was reflected in a copper haze which meant there would be a hot wind blowing before night. We had lived on the desert long enough to dread the winds which came up suddenly in the late summer and continued to blow for days, increasing the heat and bringing no rain to relieve it.

By noon it was plain that a dust storm was coming. The wind blew fitfully at first, impatient of the heat that simmered up in waves from the hot sand. Sudden gusts picked up stray leaves, turned them around and around as a stranger might set a room to rights, and then, uncertain where to put them, dropped them in odd out-of-the-way places.

Dust cones began springing skyward around Dead Man's Point and fell motionless backward upon themselves.

Later in the afternoon animals saw and obeyed the warning. The field mice scuttled to their holes, and the burrowing owls went with them. The foxes and coyotes kept close at home. Birds hid in the honey mesquite and the junipers or under the eaves of the barn. Even the buzzards, who were preparing to go south, soaring overhead in great circles one above the other, settled slowly down in the woods along the river. The sheep at the foot of the mountain sought shelter under tentlike cedars which lay over to one side and protected them as well as a sheepfold. The turkeys and chickens went early to bed. The cattle left the meadow pasture and gathered at the fence of the feed lot to find protection under the cypress hedge.

I was relieved when I saw Jean and Kemper and their father riding home. They had been working in the river pasture. Even the horses showed the strain. They chaffed under the bit and cantered sideways along the road. Jean was riding a horse that was stupid in all weather. Now it left the road and backed round and round in the alfalfa field. She dismounted and changed horses with her brother. I turned away from the window with relief when they reached the gate.

The sun became a ball of brass which one could gaze at without discomfort. It finally disappeared behind brown clouds. The autumn moon found the hollow between the hills, but it was only a thin disk, adding its eerie light which could only bewilder a traveler caught out in the storm.

The pocket hunter across the river forsook his hut, which was about to forsake him, and came to spend the night with us in the adobe house.

By suppertime the worst storm in years was sweeping from mountain to mountain across the desert. Snow and rain bring with them a sense of security, but wind raises primitive fears in the hearts of men and women and beasts alike even though they are free from danger.

No one wanted to read. The radio could not compete with the storm, and it was impossible to sleep. The foreman spent the evening with us. His home was in no danger, but it rattled with the wind, and gusts came in around the doors and windows. He preferred to wait out the storm in the adobe house, which kept the storm at bay. He was a great storyteller, or rather he told great stories. His stories of the early days of the ranch fascinated me long after I ceased to believe them. He boasted that he had lived through a wind storm twice as violent as the one tonight, but his assurance did not comfort us.

I do not know why I chose this evening to tell the story of Lloyd Randell, who was one of my college classmates. He and a friend had gone prospecting during the spring vacation. They traveled miles out on the desert, away from paved roads. They were driving a Ford across the sand in a valiant effort to outdistance a storm when the engine boiled dry and they lost the race midway. The other man, who was stronger than Lloyd, walked away from the car in search of help. He walked fifteen miles in a night and a day until he found a farmer who took him to the nearest railroad station. He was safely at the station before he told the farmer that he had left his friend under the car. His excuse was that the man would surely have died of the heat before he could be rescued. No one will ever know whether this was true. Lloyd was dead when they reached him. The man who was with him lived to regret his selfishness. I did not know him, but I know Lloyd's son, and he still blames the man for failing to rescue his father.

The Ford was never driven again. You may see it if you

are unlucky enough to miss the paved highway by a few miles. It is one problem the desert has not solved. No animal can digest it, and it is only partially covered by sand.

No one said anything. The foreman left for home. It was late, and we went to bed but not to sleep.

The wind blew all the next day, but the second morning dawned bright and clear. The house is proof against snow and rain, but no house can withstand sand. Sand was piled in drifts under the door and on the windowsills. Dust rose whenever I touched curtains or rugs. Even the patchwork quilts on the beds had to be carefully washed. It took several days to repair the damage done by the winds. We had weathered the worst sand storm in the memory of our neighbors.

Flood

The army engineers are building a flood-control dam at the forks of the river above us. There will never be another flood like the flood of 1938.

A gentle rain had been falling for two days. The sun came out, and Kemper and I went to Los Angeles. Then came what the natives call "a trash mover and a gully washer." It rained hard and continuously for twenty-four hours. The men at Lake Arrowhead were frightened and opened the floodgates of the dam, adding to the swollen river. The Mojave became a raging flood.

THE RIVER IS SAFE

We left Los Angeles immediately for the ranch, but every road was flooded. We had to go by way of the city of Mojave, eighty miles farther north, to reach the ranch, and we were obliged to stay all night before even that road was open.

I shall never forget Kemper's voice when he saw the ranch from the top of the hill. "Oh, honey, look!" was all he said. At first I thought the whole ranch had been swept away. Thirty acres of alfalfa had gone down the river. All the irrigation dams were broken, and the tule islands were lifted out of the lakes and deposited in the middle of the fields. Later they had to be dynamited. The river pasture was denuded of half the trees and most of the grass, leaving only river sand in its place.

The Mojave, which flows a mile to the east, had come to within three hundred yards of the house, and the Sante Fe and Union Pacific lines that traverse the ranch were undermined and twisted. No train went through the ranch for over three weeks. Kemper Junior was at Oxford. The news of the flood reached England. He saw an item in the London *Times* which said yeast and flour were being dropped by airplanes to feed the flood victims in Victorville.

Months passed and life returned to normal, but southern California never looked the same again.

Kemper said that there were two fortunate results from the flood: I learned to pronounce "debris" correctly, and Dr. Cooper had his finest hour. He and Sigrid Gurie were the only guests at the ranch that week. Until the day he died he never tired of telling the story of the flood. Noah's account of his Flood was the barest outline compared with the story Dr. Cooper had to tell.

Snow

I am disappointed. We have had no snowstorm of importance this year. Before we retired we came up to the ranch every Friday night regardless of the weather. The road was not patrolled, and motorists were not required to wear chains. Many nights we drove over the pass unsure of the road, charting our course by fences and familiar rocks.

The worst storm in the last forty years began one Friday night just as we reached the ranch. The storm increased after dinner. The discouraged moon withdrew and the snow swirled against the windowpanes like a feather pillow emptied into the night. Before we went to bed the drifts had piled against the doors, shutting out the cold.

I woke in the middle of the night to see a full moon shining on the snow. A few flakes caught in its beams turned to stardust. I had a feeling which I suspect might be called a "cosmic experience." Happiness enfolded me. I longed for eternity—longed to have this hour fixed forever, filled with peace, all danger past.

The feeling was still with me the next morning as the storm continued. When the sun broke through for an instant it revealed a world muffled in a white blanket stitched here and there with meticulous fences. On the side of the mountain scattered pines, unseen in fair weather, were outlined against the snow, huddled together for protection. A passenger train slipped quietly across the pasture. The steam from the engine was like a white scarf. It caught in the cottonwood trees and tore to bits among the branches.

About noon the storm began again, and it snowed for days. We could no longer see the trains. The road to town was closed. All the water pipes froze. We had to melt snow for cooking and drinking and organize a water brigade to the swimming pool for other domestic uses.

The men could not reach the cattle in the feed lot, and the dairyman had to cut a hole in the ice on Pony Lake to water the cows. From my window in the early morning I saw the ghosts of cows followed by a phantom man struggling through the snow.

The storm lasted for four days. Alma and Eduardo Ciannelli were our only guests. While the storm raged outside Eduardo told us a story. When he was a young man in Italy, his father sent him to look at a hunting lodge in the mountains which he was thinking of buying. Eduardo had to travel part way on a donkey. He arrived late at night and found a room in an old hotel. It was in the winter, and he was cold all night.

The village was built around a lake so that the villagers could fish in the summer and keep close together in the winter for protection. There were wolves in the mountains. That very winter the people had been terrified by a great lone wolf who came at night and stole chickens or geese or even a sheep—anything he could carry away. He had killed a couple of dogs that tried to protect the sheep. One villager had seen the wolf, but he was without a gun and helpless.

Eduardo could not sleep, so he sat by the window looking out at the white world. There had been a heavy snowstorm. The wolf must have been hungry, because he came into the town in spite of the fact that it was bright moonlight. Eduardo saw the dark figure stealing out of the woods. He took his gun from beside the bed. With infinite care he raised the window and waited. When the wolf was directly in front of the window he fired. The shot wakened the people in the village, and when they saw the dead wolf in the snow they shouted for joy. They dressed and came to Eduardo's hotel. Every man brought something to eat or drink. I remember that Eduardo said one man brought a roast chicken, but it was so salty no one could eat it.

The parish priest persuaded Eduardo not to buy the hunting lodge. He said the people in the village were so poor they needed the game for food.

Whenever it snows I think of this story and watch hopefully, but no wolf comes out of the woods. They vanished from our mountains many years ago.

October

I love the month of October. I do not remember a single October with a heavy heart. I wish that when I signed the deed to make a state park out of half the ranch I had reserved October for myself.

Celeste and I went walking this morning. The white-fronted geese have come down from the north to escape the early storms. The killdeer were piping their warning cries in the meadows. Their summer nests are hidden in the rush grass, which is too tough for the cattle to eat.

The curlews and the stilts conferred on the margins of the lakes and gave notice that the summer was over. The curlews will be the last to leave. They will continue to comb the mud with their long curved bills, feasting on the worms and water bugs until the frost comes.

The snowy egrets keep a stately distance between themselves and the common shore birds. It is not the season for them to be in regal plumage; nevertheless they preserve their noble standing.

The great blue heron was beside the lake. As we approached he waded into the water, and with a mighty effort he took wing. His neck drawn back over his shoulders and his long legs stretched out behind him, he preceded us to the next lake. Herons live to a great age. Perhaps it is because they settle down in one place and do not long for change. The heron will stay with us all winter.

Herons are very different from the red-legged stilts, for instance. The stilts complain wherever they go. They tell each other it was better up north or it will be better farther south.

We looked for the Florida gallinule that nested in the tules in the summer, but we did not see her or the bittern that was here only a week ago. We have seen no phalaropes this year.

The swamps were yellow with water sunflowers, and the sedges and tules around the lakes were dry and noisy in the autumn wind.

It is too early to burn the tules. They do make a wonderful sight as the fire sweeps across the water, but this time of year it would disturb the cinnamon teal and the ruddy ducks who nest in the tules. I must remember to tell this to the park director.

We have had no early frost. The cottonwoods are still green, but soon they will turn yellow and make a river of gold from the mountains almost to Death Valley.

We came back in time for breakfast. I do wish I had kept October for myself.